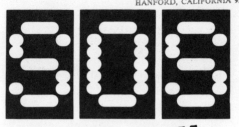

Urgent Call From Bangladesh

ELEANOR I. JACKSON

Pacific Press Publishing Association
Boise, Idaho
Montemorelos, Nuevo Leon, Mexico
Oshawa, Ontario, Canada

Edited by Don Mansell
Designed by Tim Larson
Cover Photo by Duane Tank
Type set in 10/12 Century Schoolbook

Library of Congress Cataloging in Publication Data

Jackson, Eleanor.
  S.O.S.: urgent call from Bangladesh.

  1. Jackson, Eleanor. 2. Jackson, Mac. 3. Missionaries—Bangla-
desh—Biography. I. Title. II. Title: SOS. III. Title: Urgent call from
Bangladesh.
BV3259.5.J33A3   1986   266'.6732'0922   [B]   86-18726

ISBN 0-8163-0673-7

86 87 88 89 90 ● 5 4 3 2 1

Dedicated

To senior citizens who refuse to grow old in service for Christ, even though their past may be a living present, and their present a mist that fades into a shadowy future.

Eleanor
Jackson

Contents

Chapter 1

A Traveling Comedy of Errors

In the hot blackness of night, I tossed sleeplessly on the thinly matted board bed. No matter how hard I tried, I could not free my mind from the confusion of sights, sounds, and smells that had filled that day. The city streets had been jammed with jeeps, bicycles, rickshaws, trucks, bullock carts, cattle, goats, dogs, and men. I remembered scanning the crowds for a glimpse of another woman, but the few women I could see were draped in colorful saris or covered over by black tentlike burkas, with only peepholes to look through. Bangladesh, I decided, was a world of men.

Beside me, Mac moved restlessly. It wasn't just the heat or the hardness of the bed, I realized. Back home in Oregon it was now broad daylight, and our systems were still running on Oregon time—Oregon with its cool sea breezes and pine-scented mornings. What were we doing here in the oppressive heat of this strange oriental world? It was Mac, of course. I smiled, remembering.

"We have health and energy, and I'm only seventy-nine. We could volunteer for overseas service in a country that can't afford paid workers," he had suggested one sunny day.

"But Mac," I had remonstrated. "We're too old to adapt to a new environment and people."

In spite of my objections, I finally agreed to go—reluctantly. Later Mac sent an exploratory letter to church headquarters, offering the services of two "ancients" to work in some tropical island field.

The reply we received seemed strange: Would you be willing to go to Bangladesh? Volunteers are needed for a two-year term.

"Bangladesh? Where is that?" I queried. "It doesn't sound like an island to me!" Together we headed for the nearest library. There we discovered that Bangladesh was not exactly a utopia for a retired couple. "It is a new country," Mac read, "where over 80 million people are packed into the former eastern wing of Pakistan, an area about the size of Wisconsin."

This battered infant in the world of nations, we learned, is periodically plagued by floods and storms which claim hundreds of lives each year. There are also major problems of malnutrition, mass starvation, and political unrest.

"Whew! Wall-to-wall people! And what a land of tragedy! They must be a heroic people, but I don't like hot weather," I objected. "And it's not a tropical island!"

Mac grinned. "Well, but there are lots of people, and haven't we always been interested in people, no matter what their color or customs? Let's try it, Eleanor!"

"We have a mobile home, and they are not selling now," I demurred. But ignoring my objections, Mac sent an enthusiastic acceptance letter to church headquarters that very day, even though my assent at this point was hesitant.

Then, incredibly, within a week our mobile home sold for *cash!*

"There, you see?" Mac pointed out exultantly. "God blessed us."

But negotiations for our departure soon hit another snag. Moslem Bangladesh was slow granting visas to Christian workers. We waited days, weeks, months, and finally a year before it came. Yet Mac's enthusiasm never waned. I remembered my feelings those days. I felt rootless, like a tumbleweed, rolling here and there at the whim of a fickle wind.

Suddenly, on a Friday morning, a telephone call swept away the cobwebs of indecision. "Visas on the way. You will leave soon."

Late the next Sunday our tickets were delivered, and we were informed we were due to depart the following Tuesday. Suddenly we were caught up in a whirlwind of activity—

pack; shots for smallpox, typhoid, and cholera; put furniture and car into storage. Rewrite will! Send pet Eskimo spitz dog to Alaska!

We arrived at the airport with only moments to spare. I remembered my feelings as I gazed teary-eyed at snow-capped Mount Hood, surrounded by acres of cool, green firs, towering protectively over my home city. Would I ever see my beloved Oregon again?

We checked in our luggage and hurried down the long passageway to the gate. Our carry-on luggage consisted of an accordion and three small briefcases in our hands. The tall panfaced guard blocked our way. "You cannot board with two carry-ons each," he'd said flatly.

Mac begged, "We'll have plenty of room at our seats."

"*One* carry-on!" the guard insisted.

We picked up our bags and rheumatically sprinted back the long distance to the baggage check and checked in our excess baggage, then dashed back to the boarding gate. We were the last passengers to board.

Mac encouraged me, "We've made it," he gasped. "Our troubles are over. Now we can relax." Then, leaning over, he gave me a husbandly peck on the cheek.

"I doubt it," I replied, skeptically—and prophetically.

When we arrived over the Hawaiian islands, I could see the buildings of Honolulu nestled among waving palm trees. There was Diamond Head. The mountain seemed to greet us with Aloha!

"See the islands today, and check in at 2:00 A.M., ready to leave at 4:00 A.M. sharp," we were cautioned.

At 2:00 A.M. we presented our tickets, passports, four heavy suitcases, carry-on luggage, and ourselves for further travel.

"What? No visa for Taiwan?" the clerk inquired.

"But we are not staying in Taiwan," Mac rejoined. "We are going to Bangladesh."

"This is China Airlines. We stop in Taiwan. Come back tomorrow."

Mac and I hurtled along with all our heavy luggage through seemingly interminable distances in the huge Honolulu airport. All at once one of my feet began to hurt. Had I broken a toe?

"Well, I told you our troubles weren't over," I reminded Mac. "No visas; no travel!"

Belatedly we made a quick trip to the Taiwan embassy and procured the needed visa. Finally aboard China Airlines, Mac sighed, "Surely nothing more can happen to us."

"Humph!"

On the plane our vegetarian lunch consisted of yogurt, cottage cheese, and buttermilk. Ugh!

"The cook must think I have ulcers," Mac grumbled.

Beautiful Taiwan was home port for our plane, and this meant an overnight stop.

A kindly Christian Chinese greeted us and escorted us to one of our mission hospital guest rooms.

Next morning, when we arrived at the airport, the ticket agent greeted us with, "One hundred fifty pounds overweight." Although we are portly, I suspected he meant the luggage. But, why had it taken the airline several thousand miles to discover this?

"One hundred dollars more, please," the agent demanded.

Mac had pleaded with tears in his eyes. One hundred dollars seemed like a fortune to add to the mission's expense for our ticket. Finally we convinced the agent that he was overcharging us. The Chinese guards bade us goodbye with friendly grins.

We spent Sabbath in a beautiful mission hospital in Hong Kong, a hospital built by and for wealthy Chinese. The beauty of the city was breathtaking, with its buildings perched like a bevy of snow-white seagulls on a rocky cliff. But what a contrast with the lower hills covered with shacks of hungry refugees from mainland China, and on the water, the junks and other crafts, where the boat people were born, lived, and died.

At the airport the next morning an agent measured our accordion and informed us that it was an inch and a half too wide to carry on. Mac ran to the main office for help, while I had sat by the gate and waited for two hours with the accordion on my lap.

Suddenly, "Last call. China Airlines for Bangkok!" And here

I was, in a strange city, surrounded by strange people, and Mac with the tickets—and nowhere in sight! Tears coursed down the wrinkles on my cheeks. I don't think I ever felt more alone and forsaken. The little Chinese gate keeper noticed my tears and had made a desperate search for the missing Mac. He found him—locked in the waiting room! We were hurried onto the plane. In the meantime, the guards had forgotten about the accordion's extra one and a half inches.

In Bangkok we left the China Clipper for Bangladesh Airlines. Mac smiled as he handed me a travel folder he found in our seats. "Here's a bit of information on our new home," he said with rising interest.

I can still remember almost word for word what the brochure said: "Bangladesh, far from the tourist run, has had more than its share of trouble. Rulers of the past were not benevolent. Arab Sultans made countless military forays here, causing many bloody religious wars and a consequent conversion to Islam. . . . One seventh of Bangladesh is under water during the flood season; as a result many lose their lives and homes in storms and floods each year."

Suddenly I felt sleepy. I remember vaguely the plane circling and slowly descending to the flat landscape below. I remember ragged porters vying with each other for permission to carry our luggage, and how suddenly one porter grabbed my purse and ran through the crowd with an overplump woman in hot pursuit. I finally overtook the rascal and retrieved my handbag by force, while he had demanded loudly, "Dollah! Dollah!" Then I followed Mac to a waiting room, noisy with shouting, gesticulating people in a sea of multilingual uproar.

Suddenly Mac heaved a sigh of relief, and, following his glance, I saw, towering above the crowd just ahead of us, six-foot-four-inch Dr. Johnson, an American missionary-dentist, and with him David Skau, the bewhiskered mission president, who reached out friendly hands to enfold our time-wrinkled ones.

"We are so happy that you have come," they welcomed.

"Dollah! Dollah!" The little porter's shrill cry continued to rise above the hubbub of the crowd.

"Should I give him a dollar for trying to snatch my purse?" I questioned.

"Nope!" Dr. Johnson returned. "One *taka* (about seven cents) is enough." Then, "Workmen labor all day for a *taka* an hour. The average per capita income here is $100 per year." Dr. Johnson dropped a *taka* into the palm of the disappointed boy.

We crowded into a small car. Suddenly the car was surrounded by a horde—children, mothers with sick babies, and horribly maimed cripples—all with outstretched hands. "*Taka! Taka!* No Mommah! No Poppah."

The children and the old women sobbed with heart-rending sincerity. Tears filled my eyes. I started to open my purse.

The driver stopped me. "You dare not give anything here, or we will be mobbed," he advised sagely.

As the car slowly pulled out into the traffic, I took Mac's hand and held it tightly. I was tempted to shut my eyes too. Hundreds of cycle rickshaws, pedicabs, multi-dented busses and trucks seemed to merge directly in front of us. Besides these apparently unguided missiles, heavily loaded bullock carts, brahman cows nonchalantly munching breakfast, and pedestrians jay-walked with imperturbable nonchalance.

"Wha-a-t are y-your d-driving rules?" stammered Mac.

"Oh, we drive on the left—English customs, you know. However, drivers often drive on either side here, so, we just weave in and out, and honk and hope. Don't worry. You will get used to it," the intrepid chauffeur laughed. Mac looked skeptical.

Side by side with elaborate architecture were the hundreds of mud huts and lean-tos, the latter made of odds and ends—paper, boxes, gunnysacks, and grass. These shanties encircled the city like a dirty collar. Here and there the exotic and the drab, the hygienic and the filthy, civilization and barbarity stood side by side.

Everywhere in the oppressive heat we saw swarms of workers, farming, selling, running, carrying, pulling and tottering under heavy burdens. Men and boys pedaling bicycle rickshaws taxied travelers or hauled huge loads of produce, rivulets of sweat streaming down their brown bodies.

"So many young boys," Mac sympathized.

"Hundreds of youth, unable to pay the few cents required for school supplies in the overcrowded school system, work or beg for a mere sustenance," the mission president explained.

The car turned through a bamboo gateway. An oasis of green lawns, flowers, and palm and mango trees shaded a new brick church, attractive in architecture and setting. We were ushered to our room. This was to be our home. "Tomorrow I . . . I . . . I . . . we . . . we . . . will . . ." Then my tired eyelids had closed in sleep.

Chapter 2
The Crow's Nest

We were routed from our beds at five the next morning by the ear-deafening sound of the muezzin calling the faithful to prayer. The muezzins' quavering voices pealed out from a thousand loud-speakers of Dacca's mosques. Would we ever become accustomed to that raucous call broadcast three times a day? I wondered.

We rushed to the door of our tiny apartment overlooking the city. Three stories below the whole city seemed to have come alive. "The view from here is super," Mac eulogized.

I tried to catch his enthusiasm, but when I turned around and looked at our new home for a moment my heart stood still. It seemed so dismal—two small rooms, a kitchen in a closet, iron-barred windows adorned with faded dark-green curtains, peeling wall paint on the cement floors. This provided the setting for two rickety bamboo chairs and our homemade, springless box bed. In the bathroom a pipe with a spigot protruded from the wall—a source of cleanliness, apparently. A cracked toilet bowl that leaked and a tiny rusty wash bowl—shades of civilization's comforts—completed the picture.

"Though primitive, this would be considered luxury for some here," I said to myself. Mac took note of our appurtenances approvingly—a bed, a stove, a couple of chairs . . . his thoughts trailed off. Would he be able to bridge the gap between Christianity and Islam and help these people? I wondered.

Quickly my dream-filled eyes redecorated our depressing quarters. I would enlarge the room by painting one wall with lakes and palm trees and hang cream-colored curtains at the windows. Oh yes, a golden jute rug would cover the paint spots on the floor, and tile would be installed around the shower. It will be fun to try to improve things, I said to myself.

An eager Pastor Mac shaved, showered, dressed, and descended the stairs from the Crow's Nest—the Bengali name for our apartment, we learned. Mac was hoping to call at the church office and have a quiet talk with his God before the world awoke. However, he soon learned that Bengalis start work at dawn to avoid the sweltering rays of a tropical sun. From his third-story perch he could see a village well surrounded by men dressed in *lungis* drawing water and pouring it over their brown bodies, all the while chastely scrubbing themselves under their garments. Later the women would bathe with equal modesty under their voluminous saris. Some of them would set their babies on their slender hips and bathe them too.

The emerald swatches of distant rice fields already this early had what appeared to be stooped little gnomes industriously working. Directly in front of the church the road was jammed with people and conveyances of various kinds.

As Mac walked through the compound boys and girls, giggling with exuberance, scrubbed their teeth with frayed twigs, stopping long enough to flash white-toothed grins and shouting, "*Nomescar* [good morning], Pastor."

A few steps farther, he was surprised to see the mission workers, their wives, and many of the secretaries working in postage-stamp-garden plots, cultivating pumpkin, eggplant, tomatoes, and onions, long before breakfast and work at the office.

They all smiled warmly and greeted Mac with "*Nomescar,* Pastor." Mentally Mac contrasted this verdant scene with the dry powdery dust underfoot, thirsty for the monsoon rains. It reminded him of the millions of Southern Asia who are parched for the gospel.

He entered the bare little office in his church. There he pleaded with the Lord to help him shepherd the flock entrusted to his care and prayed that the way might be opened for him to share his faith. Public evangelism, he had been warned, was strictly forbidden in Bangladesh.

Since he, a Christian pastor, was a virtual prisoner on the compound, only a miracle could help him become acquainted with and witness to his Muslim neighbors. Furthermore, he had been warned not to use the compound for proselytizing.

Devout Muslims see crime, drugs, and divorce as evidence of Western decadence. These practices are forbidden in Bangladesh. Furthermore, pork and alcohol are proscribed. All these evil practices are equated with Christianity.

Mac felt that he could empathize with a Muslim legend about Adam. According to this legend Adam was taken by an angel to the top of a mountain, from whence he saw a panorama unfold before him depicting all the ills that would affect mankind. Adam's foot, it was said, left an impress in solid rock, and the tears he shed formed a lake from which penitent pilgrims drink.

As the weeks passed, Mac saw a miracle unfold. Many young Muslims came to him for counseling. At home in the Crow's Nest, I received guests.

Printer Baroya, whose print shop was located beneath our apartment, called with his first request. "Mrs. Jackson," he ventured, "I hear that you are an artist. Will you please design a Christmas scene for the cover of our junior lesson quarterly? We also plan to print a hymnal for the Bengali in both Bangladesh and India, and we would like an illustration of the New Jerusalem to print in gold ink on the cover. Some drawings of cities in American books resemble Muslim cities with domed mosques and minarets. Could you draw us a modern city?"

"I'll try," I acquiesced.

Again a quick light tap on the door and I met the shy Milly Das, a lovely teacher of the Bengali mission school. "*Nomescar,* Mrs. Jackson, may I request that you teach art to my class in the Bengali mission school. They have never had an art class."

"I-I-I'll try," I stammered. "You see, I've never taught young children."

I set up an old table and a crooked chair under the dubious shade provided by the gnarled limbs of the overlapping top of an aged tree leaning against the roof for my studio. Mac chuckled as he looked at me. I must have looked like an overstuffed Egyptian mummy, my head bound with cloth to catch the oozing sweat, my arms swathed in towels to keep perspiration puddles from dripping onto the drawing paper. One of my feet was propped precariously on a cardboard box.

"Oh, for some of those wasted, cool Oregon breezes," I groaned.

"You surely have talent to sketch in that costume, but why is your foot roosting high on that box?" he questioned.

"Well, it is swollen and hurts. Guess it is old age plus the heat," I answered.

A little brown woman with a dish piled high with fresh cinnamon rolls from Kathy Skau's kitchen stopped by. "I a Christian," she said warmly. "I love Bible." When I expressed interest, she confided, "I am about 22 years of age and have two children, five and seven years." (Most Bengali do not know their exact age.) "It was just three weeks past, my beloved daddy died and was buried. My family did not tell me about it because I am a Christian. My eyes weep and my heart aches. Please, will you and Pastor Jackson be my *Dadu* and *Didima* since I have no family?" *Dadu* is Bengali for grandfather, *Didima*, for grandmother.

The feeling of being needed in a new country and of having a new home and a new family, with a new title, filled our hearts with joy. Secretly, Mac was sure he would somehow be able to meet and talk with his Muslim neighbors. His dream was to be realized very soon.

Chapter 3
Muslim Friends

"*Didima,*" Kathy called to me as I worked in my rooftop studio, "come walk with me; the evening brings a little coolness." I laid down my drawing pen and unwrapped the perspiration-soaked towels from my arms, and eagerly joined her.

"I can't go far; my foot is still sore," I apologized as I limped down the stairs. "But at least I can keep drawing; my hands are OK."

"You wanted to be needed," Kathy laughed, "and both you and Pastor Jackson *are* needed."

We stopped at the compound gate to watch a typical Dacca street scene. Pedicabs played hide and seek among the other vehicles. Bicycle rickshaws weaved in and out on both sides of the road, their little bells tinkling like derisive laughter. Each rickshaw was decorated with colorful paintings, ranging from tropical birds to the horrors of war.

"Look at that horrible picture on the pedicab," I blurted out. "It seems to depict a mass slaughter. And look, those over there portray sexual assaults on women!"

"Oh, yes," Kathy explained. "Bangladesh refuses to shed its memories of the horrible suffering it endured during its war of liberation. Ever since the Moslem conquest about A.D. 1200, Bengali history has been marked by bloodshed and trouble. But that isn't all. In 1970 a cyclone and tidal wave took 300,000 lives. This is said to have been one of the greatest natural disasters in this century. Yet through it all the Bengali smiles and calls his land golden Bengal, where rainbow-washed days of the monsoons heavy with the scent of jasmine replenish the soul."

"What a resilient people," I commented.

Suddenly we were interrupted. "How do you do!" The speaker was a slender young man with black eyes and a neat little black mustache. "What all these buildings for?" he asked in English.

"The building to your left is a Christian church," we explained. "The other buildings are the administrative offices of a Protestant church."

"Thank you, ladies. I come to Dacca looking for an electrical work. I live seven miles from here in a small village."

"What is your name, and are you a Muslim?" we asked.

"My name is Kamal, and I am a Muslim," he replied.

"The pastor of the church is in his office. Many Muslim young men enjoy visiting him. Would you like to visit him, Kamal?" we invited.

"Thank you, I would," Kamal replied, as he hurried toward the church office.

For many weeks Kamal continued to visit Mac, comparing the Bible with the Koran. Since he was proficient in languages, he translated for Pastor Mac on behalf of those who couldn't understand English. He felt free to study Christian beliefs, because Mohammed recognized that Christ was a great prophet. He noted the unity of the Bible as it was built around Jesus the Son of God. Although Kamal continued to hold the moral ideals of the Muslim religion, he began to feel that Christianity possessed the truth. As the power of the Holy Spirit worked in his heart, Kamal began to experience a great change in his life.

One day after studying for two months with Mac, he told his family and friends that he was attending a Christian church and believed that the Bible was God's word.

His family issued an ultimatum. "Give up your new beliefs within two days, or we will send you north to a farm labor camp." Kamal knew that this was no idle threat, for no Muslim was permitted to give up the religion of his fathers. Fanatical Muslims were intolerant of anyone who wished to abandon his religion and would use drastic means to preserve Muslim unity.

With a heavy heart, Kamal came to say goodbye to us.

"How old are you, Kamal?" I asked.

"I am twenty-two years," he replied.

"Then, you are a man. In my country when a young man reaches his majority, he makes his own decisions. True, he listens to advice, but he is responsible for his actions. If you have decided to serve Christ, don't let anyone stop you."

I did not realize how hazardous my advice might be for Kamal. I had spoken out of turn. In Muslim countries the Koran is the basis of all law, secular as well as religious. Islam is woven into the structure of their political, social, legal, and economic life in accordance with the teachings of Mohammed. For Kamal to make this decision was to reject his familial responsibility and his national loyalty.

Kamal left with a look of determination on his face. But the next day he returned crestfallen and sadly confessed, "Pastor, when I told my family I plan to be a Christian, they and the more radical villagers became livid with anger. They gave me two days in which to change my mind. What shall I do?"

It was then that I learned that some Muslim converts to Christianity have faced execution as apostates. To say I was shocked at the realization that I had provoked a crisis, is to put it mildly.

Fortunately there was an administrative meeting at headquarters that included the principals of the schools. Sukrit K. Dass of Kellogg-Mookerjee Memorial Seminary agreed to give Kamal refuge and provide an opportunity for him to study more about the Bible.

As it grew dark Kamal stopped at the church office to bid Mac goodbye. They knelt and prayed earnestly for God's guidance in the life of the young Christian.

A month passed with no word of Kamal. However, we did not worry since news travels slowly in Bangladesh. Word finally filtered to us that Kamal had not arrived at the school.

The second month passed, and we began to wonder if Kamal might not be dead.

It was four months before we finally learned what happened to him.

Chapter 4

Brown Angels

Daily temperatures in Bangladesh range from 103° to 110° with humidity near the saturation point. I broke out in an itchy rash and wondered if it was Asian poison oak. My skin itched terribly and I scratched vigorously!

"Don't worry," Kathy Skau chuckled. "What you have is prickly heat. It is quite common in hot, humid countries. Wash five or six times a day with Life Buoy soap, you'll get well in a month or two."

My rash did not heal instantly, but a soapy six weeks with Life Buoy helped. It was Life Buoy for washing clothes, Life Buoy for dishes, and Life Buoy for showers. Life Buoy in Bangladesh was not the namby-pamby fragrant soap I had used in America. This soap smelled strongly of Lysol and burned on application.

To add to my trials, I had been limping on a sore foot for nearly four months. I finally showed my "elephantic" foot to Kathy, who was a trained nurse. She immediately summoned a rickshaw, and we bumped along the road to the hospital in Dacca. Rickshaw riding, I might add, is not the most comfortable means of transportation.

One of the few American doctors, an advisor of Bengali doctors in the Dacca hospital, inspected my swollen, blue foot and prescribed an antibiotic, assuring me, "The infection will soon be well."

I swallowed bottles of pills, but my foot failed to heal. Instead it became larger and bluer. At last Mac suggested, "Let's go to

Gopalganj Adventist Hospital. The Filipino doctor there is said to be an excellent bone surgeon. Perhaps he can help."

I worried, "What could we two old people do who don't know the way, the language, or the methods of travel?"

"Now honey, hasn't God always taken care of us? He won't fail us now," Mac insisted.

Fred, a young student missionary stopped in for a visit. "I am going to Gopalganj area," he told us. "There is going to be a big Hindu festival in honor of a holy man's birthday. A Bengali boy who knows the way is going to be my guide."

"Fred, would you mind letting two old folks tag along?" Mac asked. "Eleanor needs to go to the hospital."

"It is a long eighteen-hour trip in hot, crowded busses and launches," Fred demurred. "No one can even get a seat without a battle. I doubt you can take it in all this heat."

"Oh yes we can," Mac insisted. "We're toughened with age. Just let us trail along." Fred agreed to let us tag along.

At 4:00 a.m. we were ready with the inevitable gallon of boiled water and a huge lunch of sandwiches, cookies, and fruit, more than enough for young men's ravenous appetites. I was sure the boys would forget to take lunch and water.

Suddenly the predawn quiet was shattered by the angry snorts of a baby taxi. I looked out the window just in time to see it fleeing away with the two young men. They had evidently decided that the Jacksons were too old for such a trip.

"They're gone," I remarked forlornly as they disappeared in the distance.

Six thirty, Kathy came out to her garden and saw me standing under the mango tree.

"What are you doing here?" she queried. "I thought you had already left for Gopalganj.

"The boys probably thought they would have to carry us the last leg of the journey, and since we are overweight, they left us behind," I tried to explain.

"You should go anyway. I'll call a mini taxi. I'll send the gardener to accompany you the ten miles to the bus depot to help you get started," she encouraged.

In a few minutes, a mini taxi arrived; and in no time, we, our luggage, and the gardener were packed in a space for two. Breathing a short prayer, we belatedly asked, "How do you get there, Kathy?"

"Ha Ha! We almost forgot the most important thing." She laughed. "I am not sure, but I'll write down the names of three of the main towns you'll have to pass through." Scribbling three unfamiliar names on a slip of paper, she handed it to us, waved goodbye, and called reassuringly, "Remember, I'm praying for you."

We arrived at the bus station and saw a wave of frantic humanity rolling forward, all trying to enter the small door of the bus simultaneously. Just then our Bengali gardener stepped up and held the crowd back imperiously with an upraised hand, and we entered the bus.

A pint-sized, brown-faced, little gnome who was fighting off eager seat seekers with small clenched fists, raised one hand with two fingers and motioned us to one of the board seats for two. We settled down with a sigh of relief after dropping a thank offering in his eager palm.

Finally the bus, wearily sagging under its overload of human freight, lurched forward on its long, cushionless, springless journey.

In broken English we were asked the usual questions.

"Where you go?"

"We go to Gopalganj Adventist Hospital."

"Why you go?"

"*Didima* has sore foot."

"How old are you?"

"Ages seventy-nine and seventy-one." This reply provoked surprised exclamations.

"Ahh, great age." Looks of admiration from the onlookers.

"How many children you?"

"Children? We have one lovely adopted daughter. You see we were very busy, so could not have a large family."

In Bangladesh, a large family is an insurance policy against old age. The population is doubling every thirty years.

We gazed at the unfolding panorama of rice paddies of nature's "sauna," through sweat-blurred eyes, passing an occasional oasis of banana plants enfolding thatch and mud homes in their leafy arms. The terrain was liberally sprinkled with water buffalo, oxen, goats, chickens, and dogs, but no pigs. Muslims do not eat pork.

After four wearisome hours the bus groaned to an abrupt halt. A brown expanse of a tributary of the Ganges cut across the highway. Once again a brown-faced gallant held up a commanding hand to hold back the crowd, then beckoned us forward. Now, what to do? Boats pointed both up and down river. Everyone talked rapidly in Bengali to us. They "helpfully" pointed in different directions in answer to our plea, "Launch! Launch!"

The sun beat down unmercifully on our uncovered heads as we sloshed through the river sand, making a wobbly path along the river's edge. There were two ferries ready to pull out. One pulled out. Is it . . . ?

Reading the agony of indecision on our faces, a Maulvi or Muslim priest stepped up to us. "May I help you? I understand English."

What a relief ! English! "We are going to the Gopalganj Adventist Hospital."

He pointed back to the wobbly trail. We retraced our steps, perspiration streaming down our faces. How we envied the water buffalo in the river being bathed by solicitous herd boys.

We arrived at another launch.

"Gopalganj? Gopalganj?" Mac shouted.

All heads shook sideways. Where, oh where was our launch? We had momentarily forgotten that the Bengali shakes his head sideways for yes. As we started to retrace our steps, someone shouted, "Yesh." This was the launch we wanted. What a relief! We climbed gingerly up the one-board gangplank.

We were ushered into a tiny cabin with adults, children—and flies—crowded into the hot little room. The windows were corked shut with scores of dark heads with black eyes staring at the strange white faces.

Sitting on the opposite bench was a very portly woman, with a red dot in the middle of her forehead—the mark of a Hindu woman.

"Does anyone know the way to Gopalganj hospital?" Everyone eagerly tried to help us in their broken English with garbled directions, which only confused us the more.

Just then we noticed the plump woman scribbling industriously. When she finished, she handed Mac a slip of paper written in legible English. It said, "Up to Daulaclea by launch. Then by bus up to Faridpar, and then by another bus to Shendiaghat, and from Shendiaghat to Gopalganj on launch or speed boat. Thank you."

"How do you know the way?" we asked. "Are you a teacher, madam?"

"No! But I know that mission hospital. The Filipino doctor is the best in all the country. I am a social worker, not a teacher. We send many sick to that hospital."

"All social workers should be angels," Mac whispered.

We sailed for four hours in the breathless heat. Ahead of us a scarred and dented bus sagged wearily by the water's edge. Already we could see the overflow piled on top the rickety vehicle, hanging like bunches of grapes on the rear.

We were courteously guided to front seats in the bus.

The boiled water had now become warm enough for tea, but at least it quenched our thirst. We entered a town we imagined must be Faridpar.

Filling the square and spilling over to form a tight mass in the street were thousands of white-capped Muslims. The bus passengers scattered in all directions and scurried to their various destinations. Which way should we go?

"Excuse, are you Americans?" a young man asked. "Do you know Dr. Johnson and Mr. Morris?" the handsome young Bengali asked.

"Oh, indeed we do; they are our friends," was our relieved answer.

"They are my friends too. Can I help you? I will show you to the bus station."

He led us on a tortuous route through tiny streets flanked by tiny shops built of gunnysacks, pasteboard boxes, and other odds and ends. After a half a mile, we saw another group of busses.

Again we were shown to the front of the bus. A young girl about thirteen or fourteen years of age stepped aboard. Mac immediately became the focus of attention of all male eyes. He didn't stand this time, because previous experience had taught him that a girl would never take his seat. The girl soon left, and all the men in the vicinity signed that men stand for girls—if they are in a seat reserved for women. Poor Mac couldn't win for losing.

Nine burning hours later we came to the last town before Gopalganj, Takerhaut. There was no bridge, but along the river bank were scores of tiny boats with round, matted covers and boatmen scantily clad, wielded long poles. The Bengali call these boats *noka*.

To get into the tiny boat I had to crawl on my hands and knees and lie flat on my stomach, much to Mac's amusement.

Now we learned we had missed the Gopalganj launch by fifteen minutes and would have had to wait for four hours until the next boat. The streets had no lights, and we were a bit apprehensive as we thought about being on dark streets, with no one to guide us but the stars overhead.

We rambled up the narrow hillside street. Mac stopped at a tiny shop with parrots. He entoned, "Hello, Polly!" "Squawk!" the creature responded. Mac then tried Spanish, "Buenas tardes!" "Squawk," was the bird's only answer.

By this time the road was blocked with scores of admirers. To add to the entertainment Mac wiggled his ears. The crowd laughed uproariously. Unexpectedly a voice rose above the laughter, "*Didima* Jackson, what are you doing here?"

A familiar face came into view. Pushing his way through the crowd was one of my English students from far off Dacca. We grasped his hands warmly, much to the delight of the audience. We told him of our dilemma of the missed launch.

"You dare not leave on the launch tonight. The other night two old people were murdered for their money right near here. Kellogg-Mookerjee Memorial Seminary is close by, only three miles from here. You must spend the weekend there," the student cautioned. "I graduated from that school. I am visiting my folks who live near there."

"That school is the one Kamal was invited to attend," Mac said to me. Relieved at finding someone we knew and could help us, we followed the young man down the river bank and once again crawled stiffly into the mat-covered *noka*. The boatman poled us gently down the cooling waters. The sun, weary of its own sweltering day, pulled a cloudy lavender blanket over its crimson face and sank into the bed of the Ganges. In the evening quiet the *noka* pulled to the river bank with scarcely a ripple.

We walked single file through the jute jungle, then across a small tree-shaded bridge. A sweet savor of rose and honeysuckle wafted a fragrant welcome to all. Then ahead of us in a hot and barren desert we saw the school situated near a palm-and-flower-lined pond. It seemed to us so like an oasis in the desert. Through the open window of the chapel a tuneful chorus of 350 Bengali singers filled the soft night air with rich melodious strains of hymns.

Our guide quietly disappeared into the darkness. His mother's rice and curry was calling him. We did not even have the time to thank our brown angel, but we did learn that his name was Moses.

We observed the orderly rows of youth, boys on one side and girls on the other, seated in age groups. Their voices were accompanied by the breathy gasps of the harmonium, which sounded like an accordion without a bass keyboard. Mac recalled asking a young Bengali, "I wonder why you Bengali play mostly on the black keys while most Westerners use the white keys."

Without a moment's hesitation the youth replied with a grin, "That is because you are white people and we are black."

A sweet voice interrupted our reverie, "Welcome to K.M.M. Seminary. I am Monica, the principal's wife."

Monica, clothed in a lovely red sari, showed us to the guest room. Was this a happy ending or a mysterious beginning to new experiences? Tomorrow would reveal the answer.

Chapter 5

Easter Day

Bong! Bong! Bong! The eerie rhythm of drums beat in our ears from the adjoining Hindu villages through the night. The villagers were marching, led by drummers to celebrate a holy man's birthday.

A different sound, a penetrating whir! whir! electrified my ears. What could it be? I shook Mac awake.

"What's that sound?" I whispered to Mac.

"No doubt it's a bird or an insect. Go back to sleep," he whispered, rolling over with a disinterested snore.

I donned a robe and slippers and quietly stepped out on the dew-soaked grass and nervously walked among the banana plants and palms under the moonlight. What bird or animal could sound like that? I searched the sky, the trees, and the ground fruitlessly.

A pale dawn finally sent me scurrying back. As I entered the hall to the guest house I saw Monica, the principal's wife.

"Oh, Monica, what was that whir I heard early this morning? Was it a bird or beast?" I asked.

"Neither. The Hindu women in the surrounding villages rise early before day and call on their gods. It is achieved by rattling the tongue on the roof of the mouth while blowing through the lips a high-pitched scream," she explained.

After thanking her for the explanation, I asked, "Monica, we've been so worried over Kamal. He disappeared, you know."

"He arrived here starving and ragged two weeks ago. We will ask him to visit you this afternoon," Monica answered.

My heart leaped with joy.

Later, in answer to a light tap on our door, we saw three beautiful young ladies, flowerlike in their prettiest saris, with shy smiles on their sweet faces.

"She Baptist, she Hindu, and I Adventist Christian," the smallest little lady introduced each one. "We want you to pray Jesus for Hindu girl, please."

Mac and I clasped the little brown hands in ours in a friendship circle. In turn each one talked to Jesus. The little leader prayed for her friend, tears coursing down her brown cheeks. Then each happy girl handed a fragrant flower to us and left.

"Who was the earnest little speaker?" I inquired of Monica.

"You will be interested in her story," Monica replied. "Shamely lived in a poor Hindu home. When she was fourteen her father died from a fever. Since she was a girl, and represented an extra mouth to feed, she was given to a family to work for her food. They treated her kindly, and she responded by working hard. She washed all the clothes by beating them on the rocks on a river bank. She was very careful to cook the rice and make hot curries the way her master liked them. They had even trusted her to do the buying on market day."

Usually the men do the buying around here, but Shamely was so clever at outsmarting the crooked merchants that she regularly did the shopping for the family. One day she passed a little church on her way to market and heard singing coming through the open windows. Hiding under some banana plants, she was captivated by what she heard. After the singing, she listened to a man telling a wonderful story about the one God who had made everything. It sounded wonderful to her. She returned week after week to hear the God stories.

After eavesdropping for five months she made a decision. She went to her guardians and said, "I have been hearing stories about one real God who is King."

"He is a good God. He made us, and He wants us to be good. Even though all people were bad, He sent His own Son, Jesus, to show us how to live. He died for us so we can go to a good country. Please, I want to be a Christian."

As her guardian listened, his usually pleasant face changed to fierce anger. He then began to beat her with bamboo sticks until she fell, bloody and fainting, to the ground; then he threw her into a windowless hut and locked the door.

She was given no water or food. She lay on the floor in the hot, dark hut, singing through cracked and bleeding lips the songs she had learned. After what seemed like many days, she realized she had been left to die. She began to press on the wall of the mud hut. Oh joy! There was a weak spot in the mud, and she opened a space to crawl through.

She stumbled down to the street away from her jailers. A white doctor of Gopalganj Adventist Hospital happened to be walking toward town. He stopped to help the poor girl, then took her to his home, where his wife nursed her back to health.

In his home Shamely saw for the first time the holy Book that contained the stories she had listened to from under the banana plants. The doctor's wife read more to her from the wonderful Book.

To save Shamely's life the doctor decided she must leave Gopalganj. One dark night he hired a boat, and they poled the four hour journey to Kellogg-Mookerjee Memorial Seminary.

Shamely loved the school. Her classmates and the teachers were so kind. One afternoon, as she was sitting in the dining room studying with her friends, they saw a terrifying change come over her. Her face was transfigured into that of a leering devil. She began to froth at the mouth and strike out with her arms, meanwhile chanting a strange chant, as if she were under some kind of a hypnotic spell.

The frightened girls ran for help. Six of the male teachers returned with them and tried to hold down Shamely's flailing arms and legs to keep her from self-inflicted injury. But they couldn't restrain her. Shamely possessed superhuman strength.

Finally they began to pray for her, and Shamely quieted down immediately.

"It is the custom here," Monica explained, "for gurus (Hindu teachers) to put curses on people. We feel sure that this has been done at her guardians' request. Shamely suffered several demonic attacks that year. However, each time we prayed, she would quiet down."

Monica told us that the school does not baptize new converts for a year after they have learned the Bible way of life.

Shamely's most serious attack occurred shortly before her baptism. The students and teachers at the seminary prayed for her, as usual, but they could not calm her. Beating herself and raving wildly, she ran toward the river, plunging deeper and deeper in the brown waters and appeared to be in danger of drowning.

One of the older boys had to swim after her and pull her ashore. When they reached the river bank, Shamely fell into a deep trance. She could not eat, drink, or talk. Students and teachers prayed constantly for her. Then we called for the village doctor. He tried many medicines. Nothing worked. The doctor fed her intravenously to keep her alive. Scores of Hindu villagers came to watch the girl die. They knew about the guru curse.

The Hindus believe that for every human condition or human philosophy there is a god. These gods range from the jolly, fat-looking Ganesh, with his elephant head, sitting squat-legged, to the voluptuous goddess Sanasvati, the patroness of music, riding a peacock, to myriads of other god-beings who convey curses. But the god most greatly feared is Kali. Even thugs strangling a traveler knot a coin consecrated to Kali in the cord to appease this god.

"See," the villagers would chant, "Kali of the Hindu is strongest."

At the end of the third week, Principal Dass said, "We have tried doctors, prayers, and songs to no avail. There is one thing we have not tried, the Bible. I believe that there is power in the Word."

Teachers, students, and hundreds of villagers came to see the last attempt to exorcise the evil spirit from the dying girl.

Principal Dass prayed and then, holding the Bible on its spine, let it fall open where it would. Every eye focused on the Christian book. The outside covers dropped. Leaves fluttered. The book had fallen open to the twentieth chapter of Exodus.

Principal Dass placed the book high before the eyes of the girl. Silence! There was no sound, and the crowd of people with one accord became motionless. He then read loudly.

"Thou shalt have no other gods before me."

The Hindus listened intently. "One God only, strange," they whispered.

Again he turned the book around, placed it before Shamely's eyes. Again, silence! Her lips did not move.

The principal solemnly continued, "Thou shalt not make unto thee any graven image, or any likeness of any thing that is in heaven above, or that is in the earth beneath, or that is in the water under the earth: thou shalt not bow down thyself to them, nor serve them."

The villagers were startled to hear that the Christian God forbade images. How could Christians, they wondered, know what their God looked like, if they made no likeness of Him?

Next the third commandment was read. Would Shamely see it? The principal raised the book before her eyes. The watchers scarcely breathed, straining to hear a sound from the frozen lips.

Nothing but silence!

Principal Dass read on: "Thou shalt not take the name of the Lord thy God in vain!" The curious listeners wondered: What does it mean to "take the Lord's name in vain?" He explained.

Again he raised the Bible.

Silence!

Mr. Dass read, "Remember the sabbath day to keep it holy. Six days shalt thou labour, and do all thy work: but the seventh day is the sabbath of the Lord thy God: in it thou shalt not do any work."

Suddenly there was a stir. Intelligence once again shone in the vacant eyes. Shamely's lips began to move, barely at first, then louder and louder as she began to read, adding her voice to his. "In six days the Lord made heaven and earth, the sea, and all that in them is."

"That book says that Christians worship the one God who made us all," whispered the Hindu villagers. "A miracle! A miracle! The Christian God is strong!"

For the first time in three weeks, Shamely whispered, "I thirsty!" They brought her water. She drank. Her body was dehydrated. "I hungry!" They brought her rice, and she consumed it as one who was starved.

"What a wonderful God we serve to demonstrate his healing power in that way!" I exclaimed teary eyed. "Did Shamely ever have another attack?"

"No, the devil's power was broken, and Easter Day is now free."

"But why do you call Shamely, Easter Day?" I questioned.

"Well, Easter Day is her Christian name. She was baptized on Easter Day. All converts to Christianity take Christian names when they are baptized. The reason for this is that all Hindu and Moslem names refer to something relating to their religion," Monica explained.

Now I began to understand why Easter said to us, "*Dadu, Didima,* thank Jesus, devil never never come back. Pray I be a teacher to teach little Hindu children to be good and love real God, who loves them."

Just then the clang of steel on an iron pipe called us all to worship. The daylight walk to the chapel unfolded a panorama of a flower-bedecked campus. Hovering over the fragrant blossoms fluttered strange, giant butterflies and iridescent hummingbirds.

A slender young man with a small black mustache was hurrying down the walk toward us. Suddenly we recognized him.

"Kamal! Kamal! Is it really you? How are you and is your courage good?" Mac asked.

"Oh, yes! Pastor, all goes well. I love it here."

"Tell us what happened to you, Kamal. We were so worried about you."

Chapter 6
Kidnapped

While staying at the Kellogg-Mookerjee Seminary, Mac asked Kamal to relate to him the story of his life.

"Pastor, my story is very sorrowful," Kamal began. "When I left the compound it seemed a dark premonition of danger surrounded me. I slowly walked the rocky trail to a friend's house.

"My parents, Pakistani servants, had worked for a captain in the Bengali army who was stationed there. My mother was a cook and housekeeper, while my father was a handyman for the captain. They could have had a happy home but for alcohol. My father, who was frequently drunk, fought with my mother, and I would hide, shaking with fear.

"One day the conflict in the home became so intense that my mother left my father and never came back. She also abandoned my little sister and me. Heartbroken, I would often go to a secret place and cry and cry.

"My father was killed in an accident when I was eleven, so my sister and I became orphans. The kind captain took my sister and me into his own childless home and finally adopted us, even though he was Bengali and we were Pakistani. At last in this Muslim home we had someone who cared for us.

"Then suddenly war broke out between East Pakistan and West Pakistan. After four years of conflict, the new nation of Bangladesh was born. Since my new father was a Bengali, we were all shipped back to East Pakistan, 900 miles away. But because the captain had been stationed in West Pakistan, he was considered to be a traitor by his own countrymen. No one would hire him, so our family became very poor.

"At this point I recalled the kindness of the proctor of the German Industrial College. He had permitted me to attend the college without money. Realizing I was penniless, he would at times ship me treats of fruit. He also taught me to speak English.

"I had graduated second highest in my class. But my kind benefactor returned to Germany, and again I felt alone and friendless.

"Moving to Dacca, I hoped I would have a chance for a better life. This dream was rudely shattered not long after I announced to my family my intention of becoming a Christian. One day, after my family threatened me for becoming a Christian, three men jumped unexpectedly out of the shadows and overpowered me. Tied securely and blindfolded, I was thrown into a pedicab and driven over rough roads all night. By their accent I guessed they were men of my village.

"At last, weary and thirsty, we had arrived on a farm in the north country. There I was put to work from dawn to dusk. I was watched during the long hot days, given little food and water, and was locked in a windowless hut at night to prevent my escape. I became so weak that I could hardly do the work required. The exhausting days slowly passed. To keep alive I reviewed the Bible stories I had listened to on a Christian Mission radio broadcast and the Bible studies you had given me, Pastor Jackson.

"Every night I wondered whether I would live to see another sweat-filled day. One night I heard the rasp of a key turned cautiously in the rusty lock of the hut. In the pale moonlight I recognized the face of one of my cousins, her eyes dark pools of pity and tears like moon drops trembling on her lashes.

" 'Kamal,' she had whispered, 'I am afraid they will kill you. Escape tonight! Run as fast as you can, and get as far as you can from here. Here is a coin for the bus.'

"I returned to Dacca. There I had borrowed money from a friend and made the long, difficult journey to Kellogg-Mookerjee Memorial Seminary, arriving over two months later than I had planned. My clothes were in rags. But I was welcomed by students and teachers alike. The students gave me a spoon and a dish for my food, and the principal's wife gave me two shirts and two pairs of pants to wear. She offered me four pair, but I refused because I knew there were other needy ones."

"Are you happy here, Kamal?" I asked.

"Oh yes, *Didima* Jackson," he said with tears in his eyes. "I try very hard, and I study and do the work the school wants me to do. I help the boys learn English and teach the boys who are not Christians to read their Bibles."

In one month's time, Kamal had achieved the highest grades the school had ever given in Bible study, even though fellow students had been in school five months longer than he.

When I heard Kamal's story, I thanked the Lord for the sore foot and the strange and hazardous journey that gave us a chance to visit with him. Now we could continue on our journey to Gopalganj with a sense that God was leading.

After returning to Oregon, we received a letter from Kamal. Included in it was this enlightening statement:

"Baptism was received by me December 10, 1979. Already I have convinced some non-Christian villagers to be Christians.
Sincerely your son,"

Paul is Mac's favorite Bible character, and for his baptismal name Kamal had taken the name of Paul Jackson.

A second letter, dated April 4, 1980, states:

"You will be glad to hear that I am teaching orphans of Dattapura Orphan School, which is situated near Dacca. I love the orphans very much. They say the school has proved a great help in mitigating their sufferings."

This school, financed by the mission, helps Muslims who are still in a refugee camp as the result of the War of Liberation which ended in 1974.

Chapter 7

The Sadhu's Birthday Party

"The launch comes! The launch comes!" This urgent call sent us on the run toward the river. Students and teachers joined in the dash. Mac and I crawled into the mat-covered *noka* and were poled rapidly toward the waiting launch with the invitation, "Come back! Come back!" echoing over the muddy water.

The boat sailed slowly and stopped at each peopled inlet to load more passengers. The launch was loaded far beyond safe capacity, but no one seemed to mind.

At one of the frequent stops we heard cries on deck, "More white missionaries! More white missionaries!" Then men appeared at the cabin door, beckoning us to follow. We left the cabin trailing behind our self-appointed guides, who assured us, "They're your kind, like you." Now how did they know?

A sister launch jammed with Hindu pilgrims lay alongside. On the upper deck we were astonished to see several missionaries from Dacca, including Dr. Johnson, the dentist, towering above everyone else, with Dr. Solivio, the Filipino surgeon we had come so far to see.

"Hi, Jackson! How about coming with us to the Hindu Festival?"

We eagerly climbed down one gangplank and up the other. The launch then turned slowly from the mainstream into another tributary of the Ganges that already swarmed with all types of river craft.

"Many of those boats appear to be ready to capsize," worried Mac.

41

"Some do, and many drown," Doctor Solivio confirmed. "This river has often generated death. When I first navigated it in 1976, I saw many baby girls awash on it. They had been thrown in by parents made desperate by poverty. Girls are of less value than boys in the people's mind." He sighed, then added, "The law prevents infanticide now."

Along the river shore a string of pilgrims marched wearily to the rhythm of drums that sounded like the ones that had disturbed our sleep at the school. Each separate village group held aloft its colored pennant on a bamboo pole and followed a dancing, chanting holy man.

"Many pilgrims walk as far as 100 miles bringing their sacrificial offerings for the birthday of the sadhu," the doctor explained. "The people believe that he might also have the gift of healing possessed by his great-grandfather, who was a healer. Wealthy, educated, and socially polished, this sadhu travels the world. He has been one of my patients."

The launch had docked. We joined the milling throng for a three-mile hike over sun-baked ground. Sweat poured off our faces and formed puddles in our shoes. I, assisted by Mac, limped far behind the others, dragging my swollen foot.

The mass of pilgrims congested as they neared a grove of twisted trees that shaded few of the hundreds of burlap booths containing everything from bangles to coconuts. Almost beneath our feet, people sat eating, sleeping, talking, playing games, or nursing babies, unmindful of shuffling feet, heat, dust, or flies.

We saw a woman who, we were told, had been rotating round and round for hours without so much as a damp brow. Later we saw a nude woman dancing with a coterie of nude men, supposedly worshiping one of their gods. Slowly our group inched its way along toward the main attraction—the holy man and his two brothers. We learned that these three men had fought for supremacy, almost to the death, but finally became reconciled in order to share the largesse of the believers. The birthday gifts for this three-day party would amount to nearly $1,000,000, the doctor told us. Hundreds of the poor would sacrifice all they had for a blessing from these "holy men."

We saw a small booth where the "holiest man" sat cross-legged with a quiet composure and assurance—the result of a lifetime of introspection. Large waterpots overflowing with *takas* surrounded him. The holy man or sadhu smiled, nodded, and greeted us in excellent English. He had long gray hair and a gray beard; he was clothed in a loincloth, a pair of modern glasses perched on his long aquiline nose.

The next booth revealed a black god, which had large round eyes staring into space. At his feet a woman writhed in anguish with a saliva-wet face. A man dragged the frothing woman away so we might behold the god more clearly.

Slowly we were pushed toward brothers two and three. They, too, had pots full of money sacrifices. Both greeted us in English and conversed for some time on the beauty of the United States, a place they would love to visit. Mac talked with them about Christian beliefs.

We noted several inches of rice straw underfoot and asked, "Did they lay this rice straw to make it easier to walk near the holy men?"

"Oh no," Dr. Solivio explained, "this rice has been carried long distances by the very poor who have no money to give. After this convocation, the rice, threshed by thousands of feet, will be gathered and given to the holy men."

The only hope for the pilgrim from this life of sorrow and pain was projected by the wheel of Karma, or fate. According to this belief a person may be born again and again to other lives of sorrow and pain. Thus they sacrifice their all in the belief that holy men might be able to alleviate their suffering in a future life. How we longed to share a better hope with them.

Thirsty and tired, we stopped by a huge mound of coconuts. For two *takas* the huckster would top a coconut with a sharp knife and hand the buyer a refreshing, sanitary drink.

Wearily I dropped to the ground; the searing heat had sapped my strength. I doubted I had the strength to make the three and a half miles back to the launch. Dr. Johnson bargained for a return ride on a banana cart.

We jolted roughly over sun-hardened plowed earth on the springless ride. I was intrigued by the fact that I could see no reins. As I watched, I noticed the driver grasped the ox's tail and twisted it sharply in the direction he wished to go. When he noticed my curiosity, he motioned for me to try my hand at guiding the beast, but I declined the invitation. I was afraid to hurt the ox. Now I began to understand why so many Bangladesh oxen had crooked tails.

The long day finally concluded at the Solivios' hospitable home. Late that evening we met another guest at the doctor's home—the student missionary who had departed for Gopalganj without us. His eyes widened with surprise, when he saw us.

"Well," he said with some embarrassment, "if I had known you were this determined to come, I might have waited for you. We had a hard trip, no water or food, and we had to stand on both boats and busses. I'm bushed."

We didn't tell him about the brown angels who helped us on our journey.

The next morning when we got up, sun lightened a small jungle hospital in the lovely setting of flowers and palms. Doctor Solivio proudly showed us through his hospital with its two wards of twenty iron cots each—one for men, the other for women patients—the few offices, and the unfinished wing. Outpatients filled the halls and spilled over onto the porches. The doctor and his staff provided free service to the poor, and charged the affluent a minimal amount.

I limped painfully into the doctor's office. He quickly analyzed the problem. "Not an infection," he said. "We will X-ray." A few minutes later, after Dr. Solivio had studied the photographs, he said, "Mrs. Jackson, you have a fracture in your foot. It looks to be three or four months old. You've been walking on a break."

Four months ago? What? Where?—Hawaii! Where we had carried heavy luggage up and down the stone steps. That is where it must have happened. Dr. Solivio made a cast on my foot, then prayed that the Lord would quickly heal me.

"My," Mac commented, "if only some of our wasted money in the States could be used to improve this jungle hospital. . . . Dr. Solivio's fame as a Christian surgeon has spread far, but he does need help."

As I left the hospital, I clumsily clump-clumped up the gang-plank of the Dacca-bound boat and remarked, "I'm fortunate there is no plaster of Paris on my mouth and fingers; at least I can continue teaching and drawing. I guess I really don't need this foot. I do hope no one on the compound sees me trying to walk in this mound of plaster."

Mac smiled, "We'll see what tomorrow brings forth."

Chapter 8
The Elephant Ride

As we entered the tiny cabin of the *noka* I wailed, "Oooh, Mac! We have no privacy; there is only chicken wire for walls."

"Don't worry, honey. No doubt the walls are open to allow ventilation. It gets hot on the river, you know," Mac comforted.

Our neighbors on one side (two harried parents) were trying to spread out their large family on two wooden benches to the accompanimemt of howls from the younger children.

I felt apprehensive as I looked at the opposite cabin and saw eight fierce-appearing soldiers packed in, holding heavy weapons. Mac initiated a friendly conversation via chicken wire with the young captain of the armed band. The officer said his band of soldiers was commissioned by the national army to protect passenger boats and passengers from vicious river pirates who robbed and killed passengers. I heaved a sigh of relief when I learned that they were for protection rather than aggression.

As the night came on Mac interested the captain in his favorite topic, the Bible. The young Muslim enjoyed reading the Bible for the first time. In fact he signed up for the Voice of Prophecy Bible course. In the early morning hours the soldiers turned down their lanterns for an hour's sleep. When they turned them on again, I beheld scores of one- to two-inch cockroaches skipping up and down the chicken wire. Like a magnet my eyes were drawn to my cover sheet. Myriads of cockroaches seemed to be holding some kind of a trackmeet, slithering, running, and jumping.

47

With a muffled scream I dragged my cast over and onto the deck and hobbled outside. Mac couldn't persuade me to return to the cockroach-occupied cabin that night.

Home at last, I stepped out of the mini cab, delighted at the deserted compound. "Eek! Ouch! Eek," I yelled loudly. Every office spewed out its startled occupants to see a plump old lady hopping on one foot, all the while dragging a cumbersome cast on the other.

"What happened?" Mac shouted between my screams.

"Oooh! A bee crawled into my cast." One of my ungainly leaps squashed the unwelcome visitor.

Home seemed a good place to be, even though it was noisy. A political campaign had started, and every one of the fifty-seven parties seemed to use a cycle rickshaw with a loudspeaker that blared out its candidate's superior qualifications. When these ceased, the silence of night was broken by another cacophony of sounds. At 3:00 in the morning jackals howled; at 4:00 the dogs barked in chorus; half an hour later the roosters began to crow in the tenor section, and at 5:15 the muezzin called the faithful to prayer over the P.A. systems of the city's 1,000 beautiful mosques. The night watchman's on-the-hour shout added staccato accents to the choral rendition.

"Oh well, let's rise and shine," Mac groaned. A shower, a shave, and a short prayer and—"Bye Sweetheart! I'm off to the office."

"You work sixteen hours a day down there; why must you leave so early?" I grumbled.

"Some of the young Muslims drop in to talk before they go off to work or to college classes. They are so anxious to learn about Christianity."

"All right." I busied myself drawing large cartoons of American customs to get Western ideas across for English class.

Unusual tasks of love filled our days.

Parents who were too tenderhearted to apply hot packs to a boil on their son called me to treat their kicking, screaming boy until his ugly boil burst. But adoring brown eyes was more than enough pay for our small service.

Mac was called in to name a new baby boy. He suggested

Matthew. No, there were some uncle Matthews. Finally little Mark joined Luke and Ruth in the family.

Men usually do the grocery shopping in Moslem Bangladesh, but Mac declined to perform this office. So I assumed this responsibility. I developed my own method of bargaining. Two pineapple vendors showed their wares, "Buy my pineapple, fifteen *takas*." I walked away. "Here, miss, pineapple thirteen *takas*," the other cried. I turned away and tried to look disinterested. Ten *takas*! Eight *takas*! A fair price resulted in a sale.

I shopped for honey. Two identical jars were handed to me, and I was given a choice. The color of Bangladesh honey is almost black. One jar was a dollar more than the other. Surprised I asked, "Why the difference in price; they look and pour alike?"

"Excuse lady, perhaps one jar was made by big bees and the other one was made by little bees," the vendor explained in all seriousness.

I burst into gales of laughter; the vendor grinned sheepishly. However, the devious business acumen of the Eastern shopkeeper usually won out in most financial contests.

A thoughtful President Skau offered us a holiday by guiding those with an explorer's instinct to a wild animal refuge in northern India. He realized that filling the holiday weeks with new experiences would help assuage our homesickness.

Our first stop was Calcutta, a city that proved to be a striking contrast between poverty and opulence. I grasped Mac's hand as we saw the tragedy of a dog lying on the broken sidewalk gasping his last breath in starvation, and lying near him a partially clothed woman in rags. We were told that hundreds are born, exist, and die this way on the sidewalks of Calcutta. "Oh," I thought to myself, "if only these untouchables could be touched with Jesus."

We boarded a train. Our coach was divided into partitioned cubbyholes with two wooden benches. President Skau suggested we place our bedrolls on the bench so we could rest. A mother with a baby signed for permission to come in. We were glad to share our compartment with her. But their two children, a husband, a young couple, and a single man crowded in also. After thirteen hours in misery, Mac wondered as he looked at his sleeping neighbors, who had nearly pushed him off the seat, if we had done the wisest thing.

At 11:00 A.M. the train stopped at an isolated village station; the loading platform was lined with clean-faced smiling young people who welcomed us and entertained us at their lovely mission school.

We completed our trip to the Himalayas in an ancient truck loaned to us by the school—then for a ride in elephant country. In the mountain chill of 4:30 in the morning their ponderous hulks loomed in the dark. By order of their *mahouts* the giants knelt, and short ladders were placed against their wrinkled sides. I shakily sat just back of the animal's huge head, my feet planted on the neck next to the *mahout*. The student missionary balanced himself precariously on the creature's back and tried to anchor himself firmly by holding onto the elephant's ropelike tail. Mac was squeezed between us, with his legs spread-eagled in an ungainly split. He dare not move for fear of dislodging the student missionary.

The elephants lumbered across three rivers and finally up a trail into tall, rank elephant grass which towered above the huge beasts and even their riders. My heart beat faster as I realized there might be rhinos, Bengal tigers, or other wild animals lurking in this green jungle.

Hours passed in silent agony for Mac, who couldn't move. Suddenly, the elephant stopped short. Did he see a rhino, a Bengal tiger? The *mahout* pointed down at fresh droppings, then toward a cavelike trail through the elephant grass. We stared with bated breath.

The caravan moved on again. Again the *mahout* pointed to fresh droppings. We were getting nearer. The third stop revealed a pile of droppings steaming fresh. In our imaginations we could visualize a rhino charging at us through the thick grass. However, nothing happened. We saw no rhinos or tigers, but we felt their unseen eyes watching us from their grassy hideouts. By now the sun ascended high in the sky and the elephants must return for a cooling bath in the river.

After five hours the weary explorers limped down the ladder.

Mac couldn't move. The husky student missionary dragged him from the elephant's back and laid him on the grass. Mac then waddled a crooked trail until the circulation had been restored to his sore muscles. I'm sure we will never forget that elephant ride in north India.

Meanwhile I trailed the elephants to their feeding pen to sketch three different views of the elephant on which we rode. The *mahout* fed the elephants little packets of rice straw tied into neat little bundles. While I was drawing a rear view of our elephant, he whirled around, trumpeting angrily. I beat a hasty retreat with the sage thought that even elephants enjoy their privacy.

Chapter 9

Love Story

In the midst of monsoon season we received an urgent request from Kellogg-Mookerjee Memorial Seminary. It read: "We have young people who would like to study art and hear some of Pastor Jackson's stories. Could you come?"

We could and we did. Monsoon rains had raised the river to flood stage; thus we could sail the entire journey to K.M.M. Seminary by launch. The dry cocoon of Bangladesh was transformed into a vast lake. The metamorphosis that takes place when the flood waters recede renews the earth with a rich harvest. Twenty-two million acres are planted in rice, but even this vast acreage is not enough to feed the inhabitants of that overcrowded country.

The school day at Kellogg-Mookerjee Memorial Seminary starts at 5:30 A.M. with a boy clanging the rising bell on the iron bar that hangs at the campus center. At 6:30 a.m. the girls gather together for morning worship. I shared the beauty of color in the Bible with them. *Dadu* Jackson inspired the young men with the challenge of working for God.

After this, all gathered for a hearty Bengali breakfast of rice, curry, and chapatis, a flat, thin unleavened bread, and then to work. The plan for training of the student was to work half a day and attend classes the second half of the day. The young people sang while they worked in the gardens and rice paddies. These Bengalis loved to sing Christian songs.

We watched Principal Dass walk quietly among the young people, expressing appreciation here or giving a word of advice there. There seemed to be a spirit of controlled kindness and happiness.

"How do you manage to achieve the apparently impossible—quiet, obedient reverence in your meetings and classes, but a mood of happiness and freedom among the students and staff?" Mac asked.

Mr. Dass smiled. "The best method of teaching is by example. My teachers attend all meetings quietly and are seated before the students arrive. This tends to inspire the students to emulate their elders.

"If I see a young person whispering during service, I send him a summons to my office. We have a quiet talk on courtesy and reverence. We read the Bible and pray together. Seldom is there a second infraction."

I interposed, "I also observe you and your wife work together. That is a bit unusual for Bangladesh couples. You even harmonize the color of your individual attire. Not only that, but your marriage seems to be significantly different from many of the arranged marriages I've seen."

"Thank you, *Didima*. Would you like to hear about our marriage?" the Dasses offered.

"Oh yes, we're sure it must be a true love story," we agreed.

"I was raised in the village adjoining K.M.M. Seminary," Monica began. "I loved Chita, my daddy, very much, and he loved me, his only daughter. I was the fortunate girl in our village because I went to a small-town college in Gopalganj.

Because the national examinations for graduates were given on the Sabbath, I could not conscientiously sit for them.

"Father promised, 'You will go to Dacca and stay with our second cousins and finish your schooling there, where arrangement can be made for special tests.'

"Thus I packed my few *saris,* while my father harvested some of our best vegetables for our city cousins. Daddy always raised an excellent garden.

"When I arrived in Dacca, our cousins took me in. They were kind, and I loved them for it. Sukrit, their second son, was near my age. Since we were classmates, we studied together."

"Yes," Sukrit interjected. "Monica had a happy disposition,

and I enjoyed her company. I had to study hard to keep up with her." He smiled at his wife proudly.

"Every night we studied together. Before long, my sister noticed that as soon as I came home from school I would call for Monica. She suspected that I was falling in love with her and tattled to Mother. At first Mother paid no attention and told my sister that her imagination was running wild.

"Since it is Bengali custom for parents to arrange marriages for their children, my parents had arranged for me to marry a pretty young lady of fair skin. In professional homes it is custom for a suitor to marry a girl with lighter skin than he has. My mother could not believe I could become interested in Monica, for her skin was darker than mine, and furthermore, she was my second cousin.

"At that time I liked Monica for who she was and had no thought of marrying her."

"One day," Monica interrupted, "Sukrit's mother asked me, 'Do you love my son?' I was shocked by the question. I only looked on Sukrit as a wonderful brother. How could his mother think I had my cap set for her son? I cried and cried. From that moment I felt that no one cared or trusted me. I moved out of the house and went to live with friends, and promised myself never to see Sukrit again."

Sukrit picked up the story. "I told mother that Monica was nice, fun to be with, a good student, but after all, she was my second cousin. I didn't love her, even though I liked and admired her. But as the days passed our home seemed empty without her. The things that I liked about her would not go away. Her intelligence and character challenged me. Her goal of service in teaching young people to live godly lives coincided with mine. Her cheerful ways and lilting laughter made me happy, but now her laughter was gone, and I felt lonely. It was then that I began to realize that I did love her. Somehow I felt I could not accomplish my work for God without her.

"About this time my older brother gave me some man-to-man advice. 'Sukrit,' he said, 'you must not bring shame to our family. Our parents have arranged your marriage to a beautiful girl from a prominent family with a background equal to yours.

Monica, your cousin, lives in an obscure village and has dark skin. You must respect our parents' choice.'

"As the months passed, I realized that I did not really love my fiancée, and furthermore, I had observed that she seemed more interested in other boys than me. Only one girl could completely fill my life, and that was Monica.

"When school ended that year, Monica returned to her village. My parents, thinking that I had gotten over my infatuation for her, had me escort her on the long launch trip home. After all, no girl travels alone in Bangladesh.

"As we sat on the deck of the launch, we shared our dreams of service for God and our desire to have a truly Christian home. One evening, as we sat under the pale light of the moon and listened to the splash of the waves, I told Monica I loved her and asked her to be my wife. She shyly accepted my proposal, and I kissed her. Monica was taken aback because girls are not supposed to be kissed in Bangladesh.

"When Monica's father learned of our engagement, he gave us his blessing. However, I encountered a very different reaction when I told my parents. My family simply would not accept the idea that I would marry my country cousin. I was breaking tradition. After much discussion, my family persuaded me to wait a while."

Monica now broke in, "When Sukrit kissed me that evening, I felt as if I had lost my chastity. Because I did not hear from Sukrit for a time, I thought he had forgotten me. Many nights I cried all night and prayed that God would heal my breaking heart.

"Finally, I decided to travel to far off West Pakistan to attend a mission college and prepare to be a missionary teacher. The campus of Lahore blossomed with beautiful flowers, shaded by trees, and the teachers and students welcomed me warmly as part of their school family.

"One day I was hurrying down the tree-shaded walk between classes and was surprised to come face to face with Sukrit. He had followed me to Pakistan and was sure that God approved of our relationship. I knew then that God had opened the door to my happiness. Time has proven we made the right decision.

"During those days while we were together at the college in Lahore, our love blossomed. Between classes we would walk together under the fragrant orange trees. Golden hours were spent planning our future. We shared our dreams of teaching Bengali youth more of the love of Jesus and preparing them to be workers for God."

Sukrit interrupted the love story. "At the end of the school year we asked the American missionary pastor to marry us. We hesitated to ask a Bengali or a Pakistani pastor to perform this service, because we knew they would not want to offend my father. Although we had broken with Bengali tradition, we had prayed that God would use us in His service, and we invited Him to dwell in our home. We've now been married for ten years and have a son and daughter, and God has indeed blessed us. We love our God and each other more as the years go by.

"My family has forgiven us, and Monica is loved by everyone. We feel that our love for Christ and each other has permeated our entire school family."

The story of their courtship over, Sukrit suggested that we visit boys and girls in the dormitories. We accepted his invitation.

"We do this each evening," Sukrit explained. "Some of the young people are homesick; others may be ill. We sometimes have over fifty young people with fever during the monsoon season."

We followed our hosts into the heat-laden atmosphere of the dormitories. Mosquitos buzzed around the nets where some of the young people slept and others tossed with fever. We noticed that the Dasses would walk by each bed, giving a word of encouragement or praying with those that were ill. We could see love in the eyes of the students for their principal and his wife as we passed by.

One boy about fifteen years old was crying, "Ma, Ma, I'm so sick!" I asked for someone to bring cold water and began to bathe his hot forehead and body, to reduce the fever. "Why, Monica, are so many ill with fever?" I asked.

"Many of these fevers are caused by polluted water. Typhoid, cholera and amoebic dysentery germs develop in our ponds. We try to teach our youth not to take any of the water of the ponds into their mouths when they bathe, but we cannot watch all of them. Our water ponds become contaminated during the monsoon season. We desperately need a deep well; but it is expensive, and we have no money."

"What would the cost of a deep well be?" Mac inquired.

"About $3,000, but that is a great deal of money in Bangladesh where our laboring men around here work for one *taka* (about seven cents) an hour," was Monica's discouraging reply. "However we have faith to believe that one day the money will come."

Chapter 10

Prayers Answered on Chita's Behalf

Rain, hot rain, streamed like tears down the sunburned, wrinkled face of the earth. The peak of the monsoons had come! Black mildew enfolded walls, clothes, and even medicines in its slippery arms. A pale sun peeped out from behind the clouds for a little while. I rubbed the mold off my precious pills and placed all 500 on a chair high on a table so that they could benefit from the sun's cleansing action. Later I discovered that my sun-sanitized pills had disappeared. In their place I found two pigeon feathers. I found no dead pigeons, so I had to surmise that some of the most hyperactive pigeons in Bangladesh now were flying around K.M.M. Seminary.

I shared my dilemma with Monica and then changed the subject from pills to the seminary. "Kellogg-Mookerjee Memorial Seminary is a lovely island oasis surrounded by many poor Hindu villages. Monica, how did this Christian school originate?" I asked.

Here is the story she told me.

As I told you, *Didima,* I was born in the adjoining Hindu village. My paternal great-grandfather Ishawar (God) Chandra Bala was chief of the village. In all Hindu villages the chief held the power of life and death over the villagers, both spiritually and physically. One of my great-grandmothers, although honored as wife of the chief, felt cursed of the gods because she was barren.

Hindus believe that a man can never achieve nirvana if he has no son to petition on his behalf. So she begged her husband to take a second wife so he could have a son to plead for him. Her husband demurred, saying, "I have always loved you. You are all I need and want. Our home has contentment just the way it is."

But day after day she would bring up the subject until finally he reluctantly consented. He told her, "You may choose my second wife, but you will always be my number one wife." She picked out a younger friend to mother his children.

Strangely enough, both women loved each other and got along very well. They would grind the rice and knead the chapatis together. *Didima* would show the younger wife all the secrets that would please the chief and keep him happy. Thus by helping each other and serving the chief, the home was peaceful.

One day, old *Didima* dreamed a dream which troubled her. She called all the family together and related her dream. "Please listen carefully," she said; "this strange dream has been sent by the gods. I know it. A huge shining man appeared before me. He was larger than any village man and was dressed in a white dazzling garment surrounded by a bright light like the sun. I could scarcely look at him. His face was serious and sad. He had a book in his hand and, he looked at me with a penetrating gaze. I felt as if he could see everything that I had ever done, good or bad. My heart seemed to break, and I awoke crying over the bad things I had done. What do you think that dream means?" Old *Didima* sought diligently for the meaning of her dream. She would question every stranger that came to the village, but no one seemed to know the answer.

Young *Didima* bore two daughters and one son to Ishawar. Now he felt he had a son to plead for him in order to gain entrance to nirvana. His son grew to manhood and finally married, and his wife gave birth to Chita, my father.

One day Chita lay sick and dying with the fever. His concerned grandfather called in all the holy men in the district, but none of their incantations helped the boy feel better. As a last resort one of the villagers suggested that he might consider calling the white missionaries. But the chief refused to follow this suggestion.

In spite of his refusal, Chita's desperate father finally gave permission to call the missionaries. When the missionaries arrived, Chita's father promised, "I will accept God and His Son, Christ, if He will heal my only son, Chita."

To disobey a father, especially a father who was a chief, was the most unforgivable act a Bengali could do.

Ishawar felt his leadership had been challenged. How dare his son disobey his commands! He ranted and raved, and pronounced the curse of Kali the Terrible on the Christians.

Two missionaries came to pray for the dying boy. They knelt and pleaded earnestly for God to demonstrate His power to heal and save. Chita was healed instantly. He suddenly opened his eyes and smiled. The fever had fled. His family shouted for joy as they embraced their son. Chita's father kept his promise and served the Christian God for the rest of his life.

Ishawar disinherited his son because he had chosen to be a Christian. As a result, none of the family land would be his. Because Bangladesh is one of the most densely populated countries on earth, land is the most valuable thing a person can own. My grandfather once told me that he did not know how he and his family were going to survive without land, but that since the Christian God had healed his son, he believed He also would help him find work and eventually enable him to buy land.

Chita's mother faithfully taught her son about God, his healer. But the women of the neighborhood began to harass her. "Kali," they said, "is also the goddess of all snakes. What would you do if Chita were bitten by a king cobra? Its bite is fatal, you know. Wouldn't you go to a guru, the only person who can cure snakebites?"

"No! No! No!" Chita's mother answered emphatically. "Jesus is our only doctor. I trust only Him."

The very next week Chita was bitten by a king cobra while wading in a swamp. The snake's poison quickly spread throughout his body.

Gathering his remaining strength, he raced toward the village clearing crying weakly, "Help! Cobra bite! Help! Cobra bite! Help! Cobra bite!"

The villagers heard his cry, picked him up, and carried him to his father's hut. Certain death seemed to be only hours away. "Please," they begged, "won't you call the guru now? He is the only one that can save Chita."

"No! No! No!" Chita's mother exclaimed. She pulled her sari over her face and crouched in the corner, swaying back and forth in her grief, praying, "Oh, Jesus, You saved my son once; please save him again."

Chita's father ran to town to get his Christian friends to come. All through the long night they prayed. In answer to their prayers, Chita was again healed. The villagers were impressed and never forgot how the Christian God saved Chita's life.

On another occasion an intense pain struck Chita's abdomen. Rolling on the ground in agony, he called on Jesus to help him. Very soon a tall man dressed in a shining gray robe appeared. (Bengali doctors wore gray.) The kind-faced man laid a single finger on his abdomen. His pain ceased.

The man in gray suddenly disappeared. Chita dashed through the village asking everyone if he had seen the man in gray, but no one had seen the stranger. Chita believed that his healer was an angel.

Another time there was a great famine in the land. This was after a devastating, cruel war between the Muslims and the Hindus. People sold all that was precious to them in order to get money to live. They ate wild roots and snails. Every house had piles of snail shells in front. Husbands forsook their families to find food for themselves. Parents gave their young children freedom to search or beg for food and lose themselves, hoping someone with food would take them in. Somehow Chita and his family found enough to eat.

One day Chita called, "Monica, would you like to take a walk with me? These are troublesome times; let us see if we can find someone in great need that we can help. I have a little money."

We walked down the little path through a banana grove. Suddenly Daddy took a right angle down the path toward a section where the grove was thicker and the path rougher. "Why, Daddy, why?" I asked.

"Shh! I hear voices," Chita whispered. "It sounds like some-one praying." We stopped and listened.

"Oh God," we heard someone say, "You know we have always worshiped You. We believe You love us. We beg You today, please hear us. We have no more food or money to buy rice. We are starving—please help us!"

Now I knew why my daddy had turned down that path. God was guiding him. Carefully he parted the big banana leaves, and we saw several people in a small clearing.

Daddy spoke, "Here I am." Then he reached into his pocket and removed a coin sufficient for their needs. The tears rolled down the cheeks of the suppliants as they embraced and thanked Daddy for being God's messenger.

One day after the big war there was no rice in the market-places. Although Chita had money, he could not find rice to buy. One night *Didima* cooked their last rice. The worried family asked, "What will we have for breakfast?"

Daddy encouraged his family, saying, "I do not know how, but God will send rice."

Before the next evening a young boy entered the village carrying on his back a heavy bag. He was followed by a shouting, gesticulating crowd who begged him to sell them rice. He steadfastly refused, saying, "No, my father has sent me this long way to sell my rice to the man who is never too busy to help anyone in need."

This turned out to be my father. Daddy was able to buy enough rice from the boy for our needs and was able to share some with neighbors until rice was shipped in by the government.

When I was ten years old a visitor from India, a Mr. Mookerjee, came to our village. He had a Bible, and Daddy and the villagers studied it with the stranger and learned many wonderful things. Now they could better understand the meaning of salvation, what it meant to live for Christ, and how there was to be a day of judgment for both good and bad people. It was then that Daddy told Mr. Mookerjee about his grandmother's dream of the shining being with the book, how no one seemed to be able to explain what the dream meant.

Mr. Mookerjee then explained, "This must have been the angel of the judgment, when the books will be opened." Then he read the record of John's mission found in Revelation 14.

Mr. Mookerjee's explanation made the villagers confident that God had sent this good teacher from India, so they begged him to build a school so their children could learn about these good things. As a result the Kellogg-Mookerjee Memorial Seminary was built and named for the good teacher from India. We feel that this school was built because of a dream from God.

But this isn't all, because Chita treated his two grandmothers so well, they gave him all the land they had inherited from Chief Ishawar. In this way Daddy received a double portion of land for his faithfulness. He became rich in land, as well as in good works, and all the villagers could see how God blessed him. Because of his kindness and faithfulness, K.M.M. Seminary was given a warning that saved it from destruction. But I'll let Sukrit relate that story.

The clanging of the iron pipe called me to my evening classes. There, I introduced the students to the mysteries of color and beauty by the use of crayons and paint. However, I wanted to hear Sukrit's story so badly of how the seminary was saved, that I had a hard time keeping my mind on any teaching. Mac, who had to leave the next day for his church in Dacca, also was anxious to hear the story.

Chapter 11

S. K. and Forty Thieves

Next day, before Mac took the launch for Dacca, he visited Principal Dass's apartment to hear the story of how God had intervened on behalf of K.M.M. Seminary. Sukrit began to relate, not the imaginary tale of Ali Baba and the forty thieves, but the true account of his encounter with forty thieves bent on robbing and pillaging the school.

It happened during the period of political unrest following the war of liberation. Anarchy was rampant in the new nation, and bands of desperadoes roamed the countryside, robbing and pillaging.

Late one peaceful Sabbath afternoon the quiet at K.M.M. Seminary was rudely broken by the excited cries of—"Mr. Dass, Mr. Dass, Mr. Dass! We think your school is in danger. We have come to warn you! There are many rough-looking men with guns asking questions about you. Do be careful, Mr. Dass," pleaded the two men from the nearby Hindu village who came running with the news.

By the time the message had been delivered, the sun had set, and it was obviously too late to make our way through the rice paddy and the jungle growth of jute the three miles to Takerhaut to ask for help from the police. So I quickly organized the men teachers and the larger academy boys as guards to watch through the night. The boys scattered over the grounds, courageous in their faith in God. The girls and small children were frightened and crying. Monica comforted them by explaining that although the evil men had guns, they could do nothing because God would protect the school. The big girls stayed up all night praying and singing hymns.

The long night finally ended but no one came. I then wrote an urgent letter to the chief of police in Takerhaut, requesting a police guard for the school. A teacher and two boys delivered the message to the chief, who graciously promised help. We didn't know it then, but after the messengers left, the police chief laughed and told his men that the robber band was a figment of the overworked imagination of a few nervous teachers. "No one flees at the howl of a jackal," he snorted.

In the meantime I visited the nearby Catholic mission and warned them of impending danger. We each agreed to come to the aid of the other, if either of us was attacked. We would do so by ringing warning bells. As a further precaution I had my boys string an electric wire round the school. We did the same around our fish ponds. Then we waited for the police to arrive. They never came.

The second evening I gathered our 400 young people for vespers with all lights out. I comforted them with promises of God's loving care and with the assurance that the police would come, if we needed help, because the chief had promised.

Early in the morning when the younger boys went to weed the rice paddy, one of the boys spotted a skulk of bandits and hissed, "There are men hiding in the jute."

One of the men shouted, "Your principal electrified the fence around the school. Go tell him, we are coming back tonight to punish him."

Coming closer, one of the men growled, "Isn't Mr. Dass your principal?"

One boy who had just enrolled that week and knew little about the school answered, "Mr. Dass! I never heard of him."

"Where does the school keep all its money?" the man demanded.

"Oh, sir, they spread it all among the big boys, I guess," answered the newcomer ignorantly.

After the bandits receded into the jute patch, the boys came running to my office and gasped out their experience.

The third night, I again comforted the frightened students with God's promise and the police chief's pledge.

Again after another uneventful night the younger boys went out to work in the paddy. While they were fearfully working near the jute jungle, a voice shouted, "You tell your principal we're coming tonight for sure."

Again the threat was relayed to me. I wondered: How can I protect my school family? Neither the police chief nor his men had come. "God is my refuge and my fortress; in Him will I trust," I repeated to myself. Finally the fourth night came. We patrolled as usual until 11:00 P.M. Suddenly, wild ringing of bells mixed with gun shots shattered the night stillness. The sounds were emanating from the Catholic mission. The teachers, the older boys, and I dashed for the Catholic mission, sloshing through the sticky mud of the rice paddy to help in any way we could.

Excited priests and nuns met us and told us what had happened. A large boatload of strange men had tried to disembark at their mission, but the ringing of the bells and the discharge of their firearms had frightened the unwelcome visitors away. The Catholic mission was well armed with guns. We had none on our mission, because we didn't believe in taking life.

After a long, sleepless night with no attack, I strolled down to the river. A *noka* was being poled across the river very rapidly. The boatman shouted, "The whole town of Jalirpar was robbed last night. Soon after midnight, armed men crept into the village and robbed every store in the business district. The forty bandits commandeered two large boats and disappeared down river with their loot."

The villagers, I learned, were shaken and shocked. Everyone was asking why, with the district police headquarters so close, no protection had been given. This daring crime cast a pall of fear over the surrounding villages. The president of the country quickly dispatched his crack police and investigators to the trouble spot. They probed and searched the whole area for clues, but their efforts revealed nothing.

They quizzed the police chief from Takerhaut. "Didn't you know that this large band of men was in your district?" they asked. "Was there no rumor of their presence to warn you?"

The chief answered, "I knew nothing. I swear by my beard that no word of these men came to my office."

Subsequently, the detectives then visited me at K.M.M. Seminary and quizzed me. "Surely sir, you must have heard something of this large group of armed men?"

I told about the information I had received from the villagers, and our experiences. I showed them a copy of the note I sent to the chief of police. The investigators were surprised and cautioned me not to say anything about the note until they asked me to.

Although the government spared no expense in making its investigation, all clues of the thieves seemed to have disappeared into the trackless jute area. Three months passed, and the bandits still had not been found. Then, during the evening prayer in the town of Golpalganj, the Muslims were kneeling on their prayer rugs, and a visiting penitent from Jalirpar happened to glance at his praying neighbor. He recognized the man as one of the bandits that had sacked his village. Without raising any alarm he tiptoed quietly from the mosque and hurried to the police station, where he reported, "That was one of the men who robbed my store."

As the faithful solemnly filed out of the mosque, the waiting police took the suspect into custody. Under intense grilling, he finally confessed his part in the robbery and revealed the names of others. One by one all of the men were captured, except the captain. However, after intense and even brutal examination, the name of the captain, a prominent man in the community, finally came to light. The day of the trial of the forty thieves dawned clear and hot. Thousands came to observe the proceedings. I sat quietly among the mass of spectators.

When the captain of the robber band was called to testify, he confessed that neither he nor his men had planned to attack Jalirpar. "My original plan," he said, "was to attack the rich Protestant school (K.M.M. Seminary), and possibly the Catholic mission."

The captain continued, "When we arrived at the Catholic mission, shots were fired and bells were rung, and we decided to move on to the Adventist mission. We docked and started up the short rise to the Adventist school. Suddenly we heard a raucous buzzing sound. It hurt our ears so much that we ran away.

"Knowing that my men would be disappointed and angry after waiting so long, I decided to rob the village of Jalirpar across the river. So, we crossed over and robbed the place of all the money and salable articles we could lay our hands on."

The judge from Dacca then spoke loudly, "Is Mr. Dass, the principal of K.M.M. Seminary present? If so, please stand."

The Takerhaut police chief, who had sworn that he had heard nothing of the robber band, was seated next to the judge. When he saw me stand up, he turned ashen and began to tremble.

The judge asked, "What kind of a buzzer did you have at your school?" I told him we had no buzzer. Then he asked, "Did you know about this armed group in your area?" I answered that I had."If you did learn of these men, why didn't you warn the police chief at Takerhaut?"

All eyes were focused on me. I breathed a silent prayer before I answered. Then I spoke as loudly as I could, "Sir, friendly villagers told me about this large band of strange men lurking in the neighborhood. When I heard about them, I immediately sent a teacher and some of my older boys to Takerhaut for help. I have a copy here of the note I sent to the police chief.

"We waited for three days for help to arrive, but none came. Our strongest protection was God and prayer. As for the buzzer, the robbers must have heard God's buzzer, for we never heard it."

"What a wonderful miracle!" I burst out, when Sukrit had finished. "All of Bangladesh must have heard of God's care."

Just then the launch whistle reminded Mac it was time to run, if he was going to catch the launch for Dacca. "What a wonderful God! Goodbye!" he called over his shoulder, "See you in Dacca, honey."

Chapter 12

The Curse
of a Long Tongue

My last class in art was over. The fields of growing rice shim-
mered under a golden sun, vibrant with shades of yellow-green,
orange, brown, olive green, climaxed into the cool blue-green of
the waving palms. In my mind, the opalescent blanket of green
seemed like our faith in our great Creator.

As the powerful violets in the deep shadows contrasted with
the bright yellows of the mustard fields and a sun-filled sky, so
God allows shadows in our lives, that the glow of his love might
shine brighter. I had set as my goal teaching my students that,
through the gift of sight and the creation of beauty through
painting, they could better appreciate God's love.

Indications that I was accomplishing my objective came in
such exclamations as: "Oh, *Didima*! There is so much beauty
we never saw before." It gave me real satisfaction to realize I
had reached my teaching goal in this month of classes.

"*Didima*, come visiting with me?" Monica invited.

"Indeed I will," I assented. "Our art exhibit is ready for
tonight."

As we began our visitation, in the hot steam room of nature,
an overpowering odor of decomposition assaulted our nostrils—
the rot of decaying jute in the green-scummed ponds par-
alleling our path. The suffocating heat spawned a motionless
quiet. Even the chattering myna birds were mute. A strange
premonition saddened me this morning.

"*Didima*, we will visit someone the villagers call, 'the woman
with the long tongue,' " Monica explained. "Although this

73

woman claimed to be a Christian, she failed to control her tongue, especially as it related to one of her sons.

As the story unfolded, I learned that Nirmar was born into a home already shared by five brothers and sisters. This meant one more hungry mouth to feed. In a poor family this was a definite hardship. Nirmar was a delicate baby, and the lack of nourishing food resulted in extreme malnutrition. In desperation his mother carried him to Chita, Monica's father, who gave her free medicine.

"My baby is always sick," Nirmar's mother complained. "He is so much trouble. He whimpers and cries and will not eat his rice and curry. Why couldn't this baby be like my other children?"

"Your baby must have milk and proper food to make him strong," Chita recommended. "He is hungry. See his distended stomach and how his little ribs show?"

But the problem was that Nirmar's parents were poor and couldn't afford to give him milk. As a result of an impoverished diet, Nirmar did grow big enough to attend primary school. All the little boys and girls would run, play, and shout in their games, but Nirmar would sit under the spreading branches of a fig tree near the playground and watch them with longing. He felt too tired to play.

Like a dripping faucet Nirmar's mother would berate her little son. "You are lazy, sitting, sitting like a snail under a fig tree. Why don't you run and play like the other children? Why did I have such a dullard for a son?"

Nirmar's heart was choked with anguish. He did not know why he did not feel like playing and frolicking with his friends. Tears welled up in his big brown eyes. Why couldn't his mother understand?

Through much effort, a tall, skinny Nirmar realized his boyhood dream. He enrolled in secondary school. He tried hard to study and learn his lessons, but his head seemed as empty as the gourds in his mother's garden.

His teachers all loved him because he was gentle and kind and always tried so hard to learn. But when he brought home his school report card with its disappointing record, his mother would rail in her high-pitched screech, "You are dull, you are indolent! Why, oh why, did I give birth to a boy like you?"

Nirmar's heart ached; it seemed as though it would burst. Monica, who was one of his teachers, knew he was doing his best and tried to encourage him. She consulted with Sukrit, her principal-husband, and together they found something Nirmar could do that would give him the satisfaction of accomplishment. They assigned him the job of building a bamboo fence all around the school grounds. This would be his project. Bamboo is very light and pliable. All that Nirmar had to do was push the bamboo into the soft, sandy loan and then tie with grass a bamboo crossbar to it.

Somehow the bird songs seemed sweeter to Nirmar and the hot sun more friendly as he built the fence around Kellogg-Mookerjee Memorial Seminary. Here was something he could do and do well. The very first evening he worked on his fence, he rushed home while the rosy glow of the setting sun reflected in the joy on his face. He shared the exciting news with his mother. "Mother! Mother! I'm building a bamboo fence."

Her reaction was like pouring a bucket of cold water over him. "Such an easy job, even a woman could do it. Here you are nearly a man, so you should do a man's work. What a shame I am the mother of such a weakling son."

Four years passed quickly, and it was time for state examinations. All students in Bangladesh must pass these exams, or they cannot graduate. Nirmar did not pass. When he received the bad news, he could not face his mother. Numbly he sat under his old friend, the fig tree. For a time he felt nothing. Then he got an idea. He would do something to make his mother proud of him. He would leave for far-off Dacca and get a job.

With his eyes full of dreams and his heart full of hope, but his pockets empty, he sought fruitlessly for work. All his bright hopes turned to ashes, and hunger clawed his vitals. At last a desperate and emaciated Nirmar returned home. Surely his mother would appreciate how hard he had tried and would love him for it.

His friends at school welcomed him warmly, and he was promised rice for a little work. But as usual his mother's tongue lashed out at him. "Such a slothful boy," she berated, "even I, his poor old mother, must feed him."

In deep agony Nirmar forgot his friend, Jesus. He forgot the kind principal, Mr. Dass, and his wife, Monica, who encouraged him. He forgot his school friends who had helped him. His head whirled like a carrousel in agony, "I am weak," he told himself, "I am dull; no one loves me. I'm unworthy to live! My mother doesn't love me!

"I know what I'll do; I will kill myself!"

Through tear-drenched eyes Nirmar noticed a large bottle of poison spray on a high shelf in the little grass hut where he lived. He grabbed it, and wild eyed he rushed out the door and across the yard to a little storehouse nearby and slammed and locked the door.

Some of Nirmar's neighbors happened to see him running into the storehouse with the fatal bottle of poison and the distraught look on his face. They rushed to the door and pounded madly and cried, "Nirmar, don't drink it! Let us in! Let us in! Open the door. Stop! Stop!" But Nirmar refused to open the door.

In desperation they broke down the door. Nirmar had poured the entire contents of the bottle down his throat. He was writhing on the floor in excruciating agony, with the death sweat already on his brow. His anguished mother hastened to the nearby seminary for help. The village had no doctor, but some of the teachers, the school nurse, and several of the students hurried over. They prayed and worked through the night. They gave him raw eggs, milk, water, and medicine to swallow, but all to no avail. He retched and vomited, but the poison had done irreparable damage to his stomach.

A pale morning sun rose on Nirmar's kneeling teachers and youthful friends who were still praying earnestly that God would give him another chance at life. Nirmar opened his eyes tortured with pain and dimly saw his anxious friends.

"Oh, Nirmar, you have sinned trying to take your own life. God says we must not kill. Are you sorry?"

"Oh, yes," Nirmar whispered hoarsely, "Please, please ask Jesus to forgive me. I made a bad mistake."

His teachers prayed for God to forgive him, then told him, "We love you very much, and Jesus loves you. He has promised to forgive all our sins, if we but ask Him, and He has forgiven you too."

Nirmar's agonized expression changed to one of peace and trust in the hope of a resurrection where there would be no more weariness or heartache. Then his tired eyes closed. Peace had come at last with the hope of good health when he sees Jesus at His second coming.

Nirmar's mother wept brokenheartedly over her son's death. Too late she realized that her sharp tongue had killed her son. She now dreams over and over again that Nirmar comes to her with his hands outstretched and begs for rice, but as soon as she offers it to him, he disappears.

We arrived at the thatched hut and prayed with Nirmar's mother with the sad, sad eyes, whose tongue was now gentle. After our visit, we left the shroud of sadness and death that seemed to encompass both this home and nature and turned our steps toward the contrasting happiness of the flower-laden campus.

Laughter and happy smiles brightened the faces of the young people, for this was exhibit night. Each of the thirty-five young artists stood proudly by his table of paintings and drawings, while the entire student body marched by and admired their handiwork—the first art exhibit they had ever seen.

Students and teachers gazed in amazed appreciation at the creations of these art students—beautiful birds, animals, and the lovely campus. How much better, I thought, to express appreciation for someone's best efforts than to criticize him for his failures.

With a deep nostalgia I realized that even though my work was done, finished, the dear faces of these young people would ever be vivid in the gallery of my memory. Tomorrow I would be back home in Dacca.

Chapter 13

My Brother

Happy tears filled my eyes as I hurried through the compound gate—home. Mac met me, and we walked back to the apartment past our church.

A beautiful cement cross crowned the new brick church, and other concrete crosses were built into the ends of the office complex.

"I wonder why so many crosses," I asked Mac.

"I'll ask David," Mac offered.

"Why do you have so many crosses on the compound, David?" Mac asked the mission president.

"Well, Mac, those crosses are responsible for saving many lives during the terrible civil war. An estimated three million Bengalis lost their lives, ten thousand directly across from our mission compound. Since this war of liberation involved only West and East Pakistan, both of which are Muslim countries, anyone seeking protection under the Christian cross was spared. Many Muslims fled to our compound for safety."

"Then they obviously must have had some confidence in Christians," Mac suggested. And yet, he could not help thinking of Pastor Skau's advice not to leave the compound to proselytize.

Mac remembered the first young Muslim who had visited his office. "I am a Muslim," he said, "I attend the industrial college nearby. I would like to ask you some questions about Christianity. Why do you worship three Gods, while we Muslims believe in but one God, Allah?"

Mac had responded, "You are mistaken, I will answer from God's holy book, the Bible. One of the Bible writers, also a famous evangelist named Paul, said 'To us there is but *one* God, the Father, of whom are all things, and we in him; and one Lord Jesus Christ, by whom are all things, and we by him.' 1 Corinthians 8:6. You see, we believe that one God created everything and is the source of power over all things in this earth. He is our Father. He loves, pities, and protects us as His created beings."

"But Pastor," objected the young man, "you speak of Christ as another God do you not?"

"The heathen believe in many gods; Christians say that there is but one. Look at the text once again, 'By whom or through whom are all things.' God alone brought 'all things' into being, and He did this using the active agency of Jesus Christ, the Son. He also redeemed man from the curse of sin. In order to really understand the whole story, we must start with the book of beginnings, Genesis. Perhaps you can compare with your Koran. You see, the one God has a family, not as we think it with a mother to give birth. His son Jesus was with him from the beginning. We cannot understand it all now, but we are promised that we will learn more in heaven. The Father God is the source of all power and bestows power on the perfect Son, Christ. He calls man His son also by the right of creation. We will now read the first two chapters of Genesis and talk about it."

After two or three hours of discussion, the youth requested permission to bring some friends the next week. A small muster of men had come at first, only two or three, then more, until Mac was crowding as high as seventeen in his small office. Some experiences proved disappointing, because prejudice still dominated many hearts.

In a little village near the compound, a Christian family asked for a children's Bible story hour to be held in their home. Mac asked some Bengali youth to conduct these meetings. When the young people arrived to meet their appointment, they saw over fifty children and adults crowded into the little thatched hut. At one side a scowling man with a cigarette hanging from the corner of his mouth stood menacingly. Suddenly he shouted an order that all the children must leave the house of these Christians immediately. They refused. The man stalked out and returned later with several other men, who chased all the children home.

The mob of men threatened the Christians, "If you continue your story hour, we will beat up all the men and the boys in your family; then we will soak your house with gasoline and burn it to the ground." This put an end to the Bible story hour.

In contrast, in an adjoining village, scores of children and parents attended a story hour each week unhindered. When I brought my accordion, the villagers enjoyed the "wrinkle machine," as Mac called it.

One memorable experience involved a young man who had completed four Voice of Prophecy Bible correspondence courses. He implored Mac to visit him in his home and meet his brother, an airport worker. Finally after persistent appeals, Mac yielded against his better judgment. The Bible student's brother invited Mac to enter the home and seemed cordial enough. The Muslim custom of refreshment of sweets was served; then the brother disappeared through a door and was gone for half an hour. When at last the door opened and the brother entered the room, he was a changed man. His face was contorted with hate. He shouted threats that he would kill both his brother and Pastor Jackson. Then he had muttered condescendingly, "You're an old man."

Mac tried to reason with him, but he was beyond rational discussion. Realizing that it was useless to talk, Mac said, "Thank you, thank you!" and left, grateful that at least Muslims respect old age.

In spite of setbacks, by the time we left Bangladesh, Mac could count 200 Muslims among his friends, and as many as eighteen had visited church services. The Christians noticed that a Muslim priest, or maulvi, sometimes would enter the church, carefully look over the audience, and then stalk out. The next week, few of these young men would return. This experience was repeated week after week until there were few visitors. Mac often puzzled over this unfavorable turn of events until one day a young Muslim confessed that he had been warned and threatened by the maulvi not to come near the Christian pastor.

In order to maintain contact, each day Mac would rise early before daylight and stay at his office long into the night in the hope that someone would have the courage to call on him. One Sunday two young men came in and greeted him, but left quickly. Soon after, a heavy hand pounded on Mac's office door, and he opened to find ten men, whom he recognized by their dress to be maulvi and teachers. They announced that their mission was to ask questions about Christianity. The spokesman, a leading theologian, took the floor with a nonstop harangue. He would ask question after question, but would not allow an answer. A Bengali Christian worker endeavored to assist Mac, but gave up and left, for they would not listen.

Mac questioned the theologian's courtesy and, in desperation, placed his hand under the man's beard and joked, "Has anyone a tape for his mouth so that I might answer his question?" Mac didn't know it, but touching a Muslim's beard is an insult punishable by death.

The hour grew late. The Muslim theologian handed the pastor a copy of the editorial page of the Dacca daily newspaper, which filled over half a page. He had written an article which claimed that Christ did not die on the cross, but that the disciples had substituted another cadaver, and later Christ had claimed He had resurrected.

He had read this theory in an anti-Christian book in his study of Christianity in the Muslim university. He then asserted, "I will return for my paper" and show you. Mac doubted that he would return. However, he did come back. This time he and Mac chatted quietly, exchanging ideas. Mac reminded him, "The Koran speaks of Christ as the perfect prophet. He surely could not have been perfect if He lied about his own resurrection, now would He?" Then Mac went on to explain that "some of these lies originated with the Jewish priests after the resurrection, but most of these spurious teachings were written early in history by agnostics who doubted all the miracles of Christ." After a long discussion the maulvi promised once more to return and study further with Mac.

Sure enough, later in the week the Muslim did return. Mac and the maulvi opened the Bible and Koran and compared their teachings. At the close of their study, the maulvi asked for Christian books to read on various areas of Christian belief. He admitted that the literature he had studied might possibly be a bit one-sided. Pastor Jackson showed him his library, and he chose six books on Christianity to read. Then Mac asked, "Will you please pray with me, my brother?"

"Yes," replied the maulvi, "It is now the Muslim hour of prayer. You know, Pastor Jackson, we Muslims pray five times a day. How often do you Christians pray?"

"God has asked us to be constant in prayer, for He is an ever-present Friend. I can share my every thought with my heavenly Father. We talk together as dear friends, but not at a set time. However, we might also parallel your five times, because we always pray morning and evening and three times a day before we eat."

The Muslim prayed by prostrating himself, kneeling, and standing with his hands raised many times toward heaven. Pastor Jackson knelt humbly, with his head bowed before his God. At the close of their prayer the two men embraced, and Mac saluted the Muslim with a term of Christian endearment, "My brother." With clasped hands and tear-wet eyes they uttered quiet Goodbyes—brothers under the cement cross. Unforeseen events were to prevent their meeting again.

Chapter 14

Goodbye *Dadu* and *Didima*

"Mrs. Missionary, what are you doing down there?" Mac gasped. He stared in surprise at Kathy, the mission leader's wife, on her knees scrubbing vigorously the cement floor of the church while two Bengali workmen stood nearby watching.

Brown eyes sparkled as she twinkled, "I am teaching by demonstration. These workmen come from homes with dirt floors, so they do not see the need for swabbing floors with soap and bleach."

Later Mac hurried home to confer with me. "What can we do to help?" he asked.

"We have money from the sale of our home," I suggested, "Let's buy jute-runner rugs for the aisle and the front and back of the church."

Mac agreed enthusiastically.

That night we went to sleep peacefully and dreamed of golden yellow jute rugs to cover the church floor to help Kathy.

All of a sudden, we were awakened by a piercing scream. A man's shout shattered the midnight calm. The Skaus were out of town, and the servants were alone in the house. We knew only too well that barred windows and locked doors did not deter thieves from trying to break in. Later we learned that as the night watchman peeked into the dark auditorium of the church, he saw a tiny pinpoint of light dancing over the ceiling. In the half light he could see a shadowy bamboo pole leaning against the ceiling with a figure descending on it. A few moments later two men came through the church door dragging a heavy ceiling fan. The small watchman courageously tackled the men, but they were more than he could handle. They struck him, and he had fallen into the bushes, but his efforts were not entirely in vain. The thieves dropped the fan as they climbed over the compound wall.

When Kathy returned, she comforted the frightened girls with the assurance of God's care. I commented, "Kathy, you are always helping others; isn't there one thing you would enjoy for yourself if you could have your wish?"

Kathy mused, "Perhaps. I long mostly to be at home in the United States with all my family, but I am needed here. Perhaps equally unattainable, I dream of having a set of books, like the Ladder of Life series, showing little Bengali doing things for the Bengali children."

I can think of two problems that could arise in fulfilling that dream, I thought to myself. One is the copyright laws, and second, it would take a great deal of time to redesign the books. But how like Kathy to want something for the Bengali children and to express this wish to someone who might be able to solve that dream. "Is that all, Kathy?" I asked.

"No," she grinned impishly. "I also would like a full-size mural in the church mother's room depicting Jesus and little Bengali children. The mothers and children could see it, and the rest of the church also could look through the glass window at it and be inspired seeing Jesus blessing little brown children."

I conferred secretly with David. A rush request was sent to the copyright holder for permission to redesign the Ladder of Life series for Bengali use. One morning a few weeks later a letter arrived at the office, giving full permission to use them— free!

I began frantically to draw the pictures in Bengali dress and setting. The mission printer, Ed, and Bengali teacher, Millie, translated the books into Bengali.

"Pastor Jackson," said Kathy one day, "I've been concerned about you, I notice that you have difficulty in reading when you are preaching. Are your eyes bothering you?"

"Yes, Kathy," Mac admitted. "When we were in the States the eye doctors gave it as their opinion that my cataracts would not begin giving me trouble for another five years, but I have to admit, I cannot see as well as I would like."

"We know a good optometrist with good diagnostic equipment, and I will call and set up an appointment for you," Kathy offered. That evening she and the Jacksons crowded into a mini-cab and rode to the city center.

Mac and Kathy went into the optometrist's office, while I stayed in the waiting room. When Mac returned I studied his face and knew that our days in Dacca were numbered. Later he told me the diagnosis: His cataracts were developing much faster than predicted, and he would shortly need eye surgery. Our ride home was silent. So much was left to do, but we realized that we must leave it unfinished and return to the homeland.

Mac stopped off at his office and dropped into his chair and wearily began to review the past year. He had been worried about me. I too required medical attention. I had been complaining of chest pains and shortness of breath, but I had made him promise not to tell. However, these symptoms were not improving. We must return for specialized medical care.

Mac felt he had done so little for the God who had honored him in his old age by allowing him to work in this needy place. Surely those 200 young Muslims that had visited him for Bible study, prayer, and counsel must have been guided there by the Holy Spirit.

Besides, many of the men of his congregation had come to talk and pray with him, although but few of the shy little women had come. He realized that many of them had serious problems, but that it was not the custom for women to consult with a man, even though he was a respected Pastor. One exception was a sister from Sri Lanka who probably expressed the sentiment of many. She had confided her deep concern of being a lowly woman, a nobody. She wondered why she had been born. He had tried to encourage her to believe that Jesus loved her and valued her more than she could imagine. She left his office cheered by his words.

The little children had come to him with their little problems and joys. How he loved them. Often he knelt on his office rug to plead with God for his dear Bengali family.

Meanwhile, I made preparations for our departure. Our lilliputian apartment had become home with its long beige curtains, a golden jute rug, and a tiled shower. One day Martha, one of the office secretaries, noticed the mural I had painted of the view outside of our housetop apartment to make the Crow's Nest seem larger. "*Didima*," she exclaimed, "what a beautiful painting!"

It was then that I decided to make Kathy's dream come true by painting a mural of Jesus in a garden with little Bengali children—and one little American. For background I painted blue sky with lacy clouds, green grass full of wildflowers, shaded by mangos, palms, and banana plants, a river with a *noka* sailing on it. In the foreground I sketched a six-foot Jesus smiling down on the children. I tried to sketch little folk who can't sit still more than three minutes at a time—shy little Luke with clasped hands, little Adele with tiny Chrisma on her hip, little Talitha with a bouquet of wilted flowers, two boys, Timothy and Dase who ran so fast to Jesus they forgot their gifts, and one little American, three-year-old Ryan Spiva, who was giving an apple to Jesus.

When little Ryan came to pose, he always exasperatingly turned his back.

"Here is an apple; you are to hand it to Jesus," I cajoled. He finally looked up. Yes, there Jesus stood looking down—but at the little Bengalis and not at him.

"Here, Jesus, is an apple for ya!" he said, but Jesus didn't turn to look at him. He couldn't stand that. Hadn't his mother said that Jesus was his friend? He moved in front of the picture, "Here, Jesus," he spoke a little louder, "I got an apple for ya!" Still Jesus didn't look his way. Then he walked determinedly and stood in front of the little Bengalis—the direction toward which Jesus was looking. "Jesus, here's your apple," he shouted while looking up. The kind face was now looking at him. He smiled back, and from that moment would not pose where I had planned. He just had to be where Jesus could see him.

The sketches were made. Now I must paint them in, in the three weeks before our departure.

Just then Mac entered the room and said we would have to leave before the mural was finished.

"Mac," I pleaded, "if I work hard enough I might finish it within the month."

"I'm so sorry, dear, but something has happened that changes our plans. Mr. Edwards, the mission treasurer, just told me the air companies are raising their fares. Unless we leave next week, our tickets to the States will cost two or three hundred dollars extra."

"Oh no! I can't paint it in that short a time," I wailed.

"Do the best you can; I'm sure that they will appreciate anything you do."

From early morning to late at night I painted on that picture. I got paint in my hair, and spattered it on my skin and clothes, but the work progressed. Meanwhile Mac set aside books from his beloved library to leave with the church and packed our few belongings.

The fateful day of separation arrived too rapidly. The crochety old mission bus stood waiting to carry us to the airport. Two hours before departure time I was still painting madly, and Mac was doing last minute work in his church office, when he looked at his watch and realized we had reached our deadline and we sprinted home.

The open door of the apartment revealed both the small bedroom and living room packed with church friends who had come to bid us farewell. We greeted everyone and crowded into the bathroom to change. Mac snapped the suitcases shut while I dropped my paint spattered clothes in the waste basket, closed the door of the Crow's Nest, and descended the ancient stairs for the last time.

"Goodbye Pastor! Goodbye Pastor!" our Bengali friends shouted. Many of them had gathered under the mango tree. Their colorful saris made it look like a garden of bright-hued flowers with their children clustered around them like flower buds. I rushed over to them to bid them goodbye. "I know it isn't your custom," I said, "but may I give you an American kiss of farewell?" Shy smiles and each brown cheek was raised for the damp, teary American salute. "You will all meet me in the earth made new, won't you?" Brown faces broke into smiles, and black heads nodded in assent.

The men and boys crowded around the bus while *Dadu* Jackson clasped the dear brown hands for the last time. "Goodbye Pastor! Goodbye!" They waved as long as the bus was in sight.

"O God, take care of our Bengali family," Mac prayed as the bus turned the bend.